Leaders
Around Me:
Autobiographies of Autistics who Type, Point, & Spell to Communicate

Edited by

EDLYN VALLEJO PEÑA, Ph.D.

D1366255

DEDICATION

This book is dedicated to all the authors of this book.
I value the courage and advocacy it takes to share your
personal stories.

CONTENTS

Featured in Films and Documentaries

Innovators, Founders, and Creators

University and College Students

Educational Inclusion Advocates

Community Inclusion Advocates

ACKNOWLEDGMENTS

I am grateful for all the authors who wrote and submitted their autobiographical narratives for this book project. Your stories are simply beautiful. Your experiences will undoubtedly educate and encourage other nonspeaking and minimally speaking individuals around the globe!

I could not have put this book together without the assistance of my research assistant, Sara Cook. Thank you for the many hours you invested and your attention to detail. Thank you to Sunnie Schearer of Schearer Designs for designing a gorgeous book cover.

Last but not least, thank you to my dear family. My son, Diego Peña, is a force of nature. His insights, wit, and eloquence never cease to amaze me. Thank you for contributing to the preface of *Leaders Around Me*. My husband, Dr. Damien Peña, is patient, supportive, and understanding through every professional adventure I undertake, including organizing the publication of this book. Thank you for loving me unconditionally.

PREFACE

Leaders Around Me: Autobiographies of Autistics who Type, Point, and Spell to Communicate is a compilation of 45 autobiographies of extraordinary individuals who use keyboards, letter boards, and communication devices. The idea for *Leaders Around Me* came to me one day when reflecting on the social experiences of my son, Diego. Diego is a nonspeaking young man who has been fortunate to grow up with friends who also type and spell to communicate like himself. Since I co-founded the Autism and Communication Center (ACC) at California Lutheran University in 2016, a robust community of people who type and spell to communicate has formed in our region. This community has been a life force for Diego. He has autistic mentors and friends with whom he interacts on a regular basis at ACC events. However, I realize Diego is privileged for growing up under these circumstances. Diego and his community of friends are exceptions to the status quo. In many places around the world, established communities of people who use augmentative and alternative communication are rare. More often than not, nonspeaking and minimally speaking individuals, their families, and the professionals who support them have little to no sources of social and communication supports.

Fortunately, individuals without communities and friends of people who use letter boards, keyboards, and tablets have been able to draw strength from published memoirs written by nonspeaking and minimally speaking autistic advocates. These include powerful books such as *How Can I Talk if my Lips Don't Move?* by Tito Mukhopadhyay, *Ido in Autismland* by Ido Kedar, *The Reason I Jump* by Naoki Higashida, and *Anatomy of Autism* by Diego Peña. *Leaders Around Me* will surely serve as another source of education, inspiration, and hope for the nonspeaking and minimally speaking community. Diego argues that the book "is also important because very unique autistics have a chance to dazzle the world."

In their autobiographical narratives, authors of all ages touch on common challenges faced by autistics who type and spell to communicate, including educational segregation, motor and sensory difficulties, presumed incompetence, and lack of access to communication in schools. In the face of these personal and societal barriers, the authors prevail. The autobiographies shine with examples of resilience, accomplishments, and achievements. They demonstrate that with the right supports and resources, anything is possible. By reading the authors' stories, nonspeaking and minimally speaking readers will realize they are, in fact, surrounded by friends, mentors, and leaders who experience the world just like them. Each autobiography ends with questions to encourage reader engagement and reflection.

Diego concludes that by reading *Leaders Around Me*, "People can learn that there is hope no matter the challenges you face. There is hope for a real life and for people to never count you out. If I had a book like this, I would know that I was never alone. Autism is a lonely experience, but remember you have friends all across the world that know exactly how you feel. Never stop fighting for your place in this world. I am here for you, my fellow warriors. Love yourself always."

BOOK AUTHORS AND BLOGGERS

1 NIKO BOSKOVIC

Niko Boskovic
Oregon
18 years old

Highlights:
- Blogger at
  https://www.facebook.com/nikoboskovicPDX
  and writes monthly column for Oregon Council
  on Developmental Disabilities:
  https://www.ocdd.org/nikos-blog/
- First student in his school district to communicate
  with a letterboard
- Works part-time at Trader Joe's

Having the opportunity to share more about my
personal experiences with being autistic is a bit like pulling
on a loose thread of a sweater and finding that instead of
unraveling the whole thing, you only made a big hole in the
middle. It seems unlikely that I will be able to eloquently
describe it in any way that does it justice. However, I believe
that the more we listen to people who live without shame

or regret at being autistic, the more likely it is that future generations of autistics will be better supported in their schools and communities.

I wanted so many times to be accepted for who I was instead of feeling like I had to fix what was wrong with me. It's not fair to make a child feel this way, but I know my parents didn't mean it to be a punishment. Rather, they wanted to help me connect with them and be able to navigate this confusing world. In a way, I guess all that therapy worked, but I wonder where I would have been if I had been left on my own developmental track. It doesn't really matter, though, because I really like my life now. Having gained a method of communication has made all the difference in the world.

Before I was able to communicate, I had to do whatever anyone else thought I should do; once I could letterboard, I could have a say in my life and the way I spent my free time. Before I could communicate my thoughts, I was treated like I was not very intelligent; after I learned how to connect letters on a board, my intelligence was no longer questioned because I proved it daily. I learned how to open the world with my thoughts, and was met with high expectations for my future. All this was so unbelievable and unlikely that I don't ever take it for granted. It seems unlikely that I will ever speak clearly or eloquently, so I continue to work on my independent typing as a long-term goal. It has been my goal for four years, and I will eventually get there.

It has to be said that I wouldn't change or give up any portion of my autism for any reason that some people might think up. In fact, I am so glad to have it! It had made my life so interesting and rich in experience, and I honestly feel lucky. Having autism is just another way of looking at the world, and we need to make room for our voices to be heard—not just our parents' voices, but ours as well. Ours are most important to be heard, of course.

That so many parents drown out their kids' voices is a tragedy. Things must evolve so that more of us can affect change in our lives and improve circumstances for the future. It should be every parent's goal for their autistic child to be as independent as possible, however impacted they are. Having this as a goal doesn't mean ignoring the difficulties parents have in raising an autistic son or daughter, but too many get caught up in the challenges and get beat down in the process. Where's the opportunity for change? I was little when I saw my parents get so run down and beaten by all that they were trying to do for me. I thought there was something really wrong with me to make them so stressed. It still bums me out to this day to think about those times.

That we continue to isolate autistics from the general public is only reinforcing decades-old stereotypes about people with disabilities. As my mom shared with me recently, if I had been born twenty years ago, she and my father would have undoubtedly been advised to put me in an institution and forget about me. Are we really that far away from those days? Thankfully, I think we are. I can say with confidence that I used to be the first student who communicates via letterboard in my school district, but I don't think I will be the last. I feel it's so important to be seen out in the community using the letterboard and normalizing people like me going about their business. We need to be everywhere all the time so that people get used to us. I'm so lucky that my family believes this, and puts it into practice every day. It's my belief that we will see a groundswell of change in the coming years where people with disabilities will take a central role in determining what issues are important to their very existence, like what they want to do for work, where they want to live, how they choose to spend their time and with whom. Such basic choices, but often out of reach for people like me. It should come naturally, and yet these rights are revolutionary when applied to autistics. I feel so lucky to be alive at a time when our movement is gaining its legs, and we stand alongside our parents instead of behind them.

Reflection Questions:
1. Niko describes being lucky and experiencing the world more richly because of his autism. What advantages or benefits have you experienced from being autistic?
2. Niko advocates for the public to listen to autistic voices, not just those of parents. Describe ways in which you would spread your message or amplify your voice so that others will listen.

2 ROHIT DIXIT
BREAKING THE BARRIERS

Rohit V. Dixit
California
22 years old

Highlights:
- Blogger at www.autismfunstories.worldpress.com
- Enjoys participating in an adult day program
- Aspires to be a journalist

Earlier people with autism were treated differently and looked stereotypical. After the advancement of therapies along with improvement in technological innovation, more doors opened for opportunities as well as towards better understanding. I am one of the living examples. I have to tell you it is not a cakewalk to go through all of the therapy but at the same time can be done. Early childhood intervention made all the difference for me.

Let me tell you something about myself first. I was born on June 23rd, 1996 in Portland OR. I met all my early milestones at the right age. My parents noticed the delay in speech along with other symptoms, which were major concerns and none of the pediatricians could diagnose properly. I got official diagnosis as well as the label autism spectrum when I was 3 ½ years old after we moved to California. I was aloof all the time. During my childhood I had no friends nor was I into playing. I never went to movies or theme parks mainly because of the noise and the crowds. The experience was like going into a Hard Rock Cafe with banging music. My parents had no clue what caused my behavior. They read books, attended autism conferences to understand my behavior, and provide the necessary intervention. They used various means to communicate. Even though I recognized alphabets and numbers, it was hard for me to convey what they meant to me and resulted in a vacuum leading to frustration and aggression. On top of this, when people started talking about my drawbacks, I felt like shouting. I was telling myself, one day I will tell my story (through a different mode). That day came in the year 2003 when I met Soma, through my first session of rapid prompting method (RPM).

My parents heard about Soma Mukhopadhyay while attending an autism conference in 2001. Soma created a technique RPM which uses continuous prompts and the student is asked questions and also provided answers (also called a "teach and ask" paradigm). I began to attend Soma's sessions when she had her clinic in Burbank, CA; that time I was 7 years old. Our first session was so enchanting that I opened up perfectly to her. Her sweet voice was so appealing to connect with her. The tearing of paper sound was so funny that made me focus on what she was talking. She is the best teacher to teach age appropriate topics that fused interest and made me learn rapidly. Then my mom started the same thing. It took me some time to build the rapport with my mom and after few months, I made the connection.

I have a hard time to generalize communication with others like my teachers, therapists and aids. One of the main difficulties is getting a comfort feeling with others. Over the time I got more comfortable with my teachers, aids and therapists. They started believing in my ability to learn. My parents put it in the IEP to teach age appropriate grade level curriculum. I was main-streamed into regular classes at school with an aide sitting next to me and my mom trained the aide. In high school I was mainstreamed in 5 subjects: Algebra, Economics, Government, Consumer Math, and History. I was more interested in history because learning the past is always fascinating and helps to mold our future. I graduated from high school in 2014. I was enrolled in an adult transition program after High School and I graduated from the adult program in 2018. I have now joined an adult day program and I am enjoying every bit. I love to attend collage but I cannot sit for a long time. I get very restless and lose my attention. I have decided to study journalism through online courses.

I started my travel logs and commented on current affairs. You can find my articles in my blog site below. I started my writing journey towards the end of 2003 with short stories (about a paragraph). Previously in 2012, I got one of my articles published in the community yearly publication of our South Asian support group "Jeena" which was well received with appreciation and encouragement. By 2013, I was able to contribute another article to our community's yearly publication. Having published my first article in our community annual publication was one of my proud achievements. I have been contributing to a couple more publications annually. My ambition is to be a full-fledged journalist one day with the help of God.

I have come across so many people who have inspired me, like my high school teacher Miss Stevens, my aides and few of my therapists, one of them being the best speech therapist (Darlene Hanson from REACH). All of them have guided me through the right channels and this had an immense effect on me. I have to add my maternal uncle

Guru and aunt Megha were also a big source of inspiration. Parents of our support group (Jeena SoCal) were always there to encourage me and of course my friends with whom I always have fun. I will be remiss if I don't add the contribution of my parents who have supported, nourished, and encouraged me to work on to achieve my dream goal of becoming a free-lance journalist. Of course I still have a long way to go to accomplish my goal, my main challenges being the mind and body coordination, I struggle to focus to finish any work and need continuous prompting.

Today there are many resources at our disposal; technology is our best friend. Please make use of it. People are differently molded, not just special needs, but everybody living on this planet. Some are slow and some are fast. Everybody reaches goals at his or her own pace. I want to tell the future generations to follow your dream. Life is beautiful; enjoy and be in a constant journey to acquire the knowledge that the world is offering. Never give up the practice of spelling, typing, and communicating so that world can hear your voices through your writing.

Here is the link of my blog. Your valuable comments and suggestions appreciated.
www.autismfunstories.worldpress.com

Reflection Questions:
1. Rohit explains that in his writings he has written travel logs. Write a log about your favorite vacation or trip. What did you do and what made it special?
2. Rohit says that "technology is our best friend." How has technology been a good friend to you? What are the advantages and disadvantages of technology?

3 RISHI JENA

Rishi Jena
Georgia
15 years old

Highlights:
- Blogger at https://sherriebanerjee.wordpress.com
- Winner of writing contest for the state of Georgia
- Gifted in math, and working on Advanced Placement Calculus using the letter board

I am Rishi Jena, 15 years old and most of my life has been spent in the powerful reality that I am unable to communicate reliably. In 2016, I was introduced to the letter board where I was able to spell out my thoughts for the first time. It gave me freedom from the excruciatingly painful world of silence after twelve years. Finally, everyone could realize how talented and gifted I am and how expressively I can write.

My life changed dramatically after learning to communicate. From being told that I am extremely cognitively impaired in 5th grade, to being transferred to middle school with age appropriate curriculum and inclusion in Math classes. I also had access to a keyboard and a communication partner in school. It was an exhilarating time to be recognized for my talents rather than my disability. This was all possible due to the untiring efforts of my parents and my lawyer, Janet Preston, who fought for 10 hours in an IEP meeting to make the significant difference in my life.

Inclusion in age-appropriate curriculum and community acceptance are my happiest milestones after keyboarding. To have the label of being cognitively impaired, removed from the school environment after a decade, is the feather in my cap. I participated in a Reflections nation-wide writing completion in school in fall of 2016. My story received First Place at the state level which boosted my self-esteem tremendously. I also started writing a blog which touched a lot of hearts (https://sherriebanerjee.wordpress.com/). I participated in middle school PE and Chorus classes like all typical teenagers for the last three years. I started attending Sunday social studies classes with typical teenagers in 2017 fall and really enjoyed them. The teacher and classmates accepted me just the way I am and I also got up on stage to act in a play last year with some vibrant teenagers. I did not want to use the letter-board in front of a large audience and practiced my line over and over again. I was successful in getting up on stage to say my line and many audience participants cheered me for the effort. These experiences are instrumental in building up my confidence for an inclusive future.

When I started middle school, I was mostly non-verbal and communicating using the keyboard. However, after attending inclusion classes I felt a fire light under me to talk and now I am able to verbally answer the majority of academic questions in school. My mother also enrolled me in online high school in 2018 so I can earn a degree faster, I listen to the videos and answer the majority of high school questions verbally as well. It is very encouraging to overcome severe speech delays since childhood and currently have the verbal clarity to answer academic and social questions.

Parents are the greatest support I have experienced in my life. Both my parents work tirelessly every day so I can aspire for higher goals in life. My mother is an inspiring force propelling me to greater heights daily. My father has the highest work ethic that I have ever seen. Unconditional love and support can alter anyone's life at any time.

Many mentors have given their heart and soul to enable me to have a presence in the community. These mentors are the driving force behind my inclusion. Ms. Jess Sibley taught me spelling to communicate and is exceptionally gifted in teaching kids like me to use the keyboard. Ms. Bryana is very positive and encouraging to convert my typing to speech. Ms. Jen Leon unlocked my unique gift with Math and starting teaching me advanced Calculus which is very enjoyable and exciting. Mr Nesbitt, my high school teacher is a true inspiration on how to go above and beyond to regulate and teach students with motor differences. Mr. Suri, the teacher in Sunday inclusion classes is my mentor for community inclusion. I have participated in many community programs and fields trips with his encouragement. Ms. Anthonette helps me at home to practice motor skills and daily living skills so I can eventually go to college and lead an independent life.

I am very persevering and motivated for success in life. I try to maintain a growth mindset during challenging days to keep myself motivated for better days ahead. Growth mindset helps me believe that I can learn the skills to self-regulate in the near future. Success means plenty of recognition in the field of math and science. Math is very fascinating and thoroughly enjoyable. I like to solve math problems for fun and leisure activities. I am also a typical teenager and enjoy dances with pretty girls, movies, swimming, working out at the gym and playing the piano.

My connection to a Higher Power is very powerful and levitates me to different position than most others even in difficult circumstances. I see my disability as a higher calling to achieve more than average.

To live a life without fear is a blessing; this blessing comes after a lot of prayers, discipline, and good deeds for those in need. A calm mind, healthy body, and submission to a Higher Power are in my opinion the top qualities to lead a peaceful life. Life is a blissful experience without the pervasive intrusion of fear. I try daily to chant OM 25 times to calm my body and mind in difficult circumstances. The perfect life would also be filled with academic success and personal growth in independent living. I also want to participate in inclusion programs and represent the special needs community. I would like to be married to a beautiful girl who is kind and patient.

The leaders of society equate intelligence to talking verbally. I want to change their notions with success in academics and social inclusion. I will raise my emerging voice and fight for all non-verbal children to be provided with a good education and social acceptance for their intelligence.

Reflection Questions:
1. In the last few years, Rishi has been involved in a number of inclusive extracurricular activities such as entering writing contests and acting in a play. What kinds of inclusive extracurricular activities are you proud of or hope to participate in the future?
2. Rishi says that "to live a life without fear is a blessing." He suggests ways in which to conquer fear and live a peaceful life. What strategies have you successfully used to conquer your fears and bring yourself peace?

4 IDO KEDAR

Ido Kedar
California
23 years old

Highlights:

- Author of critically acclaimed *Ido in Autismland* (2014) and *In Two Worlds* (2018)
- Presented at UN 2019 International Autism Day and many other conferences
- Writings featured in media (including Wall Street Journal, Los Angeles Times, NBC News, Atlantic Magazine)

My story is probably similar to many in this book. I was not able to demonstrate my intelligence for many years in spite of extensive therapies of the usual sort, primarily applied behavioral analysis [ABA], speech and OT. I have written a great deal in my books and my blog about how awful these years were in so many ways. The issue was not kindliness or earnestness because the many therapists and behaviorists who entered my life were usually chipper and cheerful, like a bunch of Disney characters. It was part of the therapy, to be perfectly honest. They were chipper and cheery while flipping flashcards in repetitive drills that numbed my brain with boredom.

It is recommended in ABA to give 40 hours a week of this stuff. "Touch your nose!" "Touch table!" "Touch apple!" "No, try again!" "High five!" The artificial simplified speech, plus the boredom made me terribly frustrated, but that wasn't the worst of it. The worst of it was that these drills were a waste of time, effort and emotional energy, not to mention money. I started just before my third birthday and finished when my team refused to believe I could understand and communicate at the age of seven. That is a lot of "Touch your nose!" commands.

The problem was that my earnest educators taught me like I was kind of a thick toddler who didn't understand words. They were totally wrong in every respect. My disability is not a receptive language problem nor a cognition problem, which all my instruction was designed to fix in tiny increments. Rather, my understanding was excellent and my intelligence I hope is above average. I know you have read this on page after page already. It's not cognitive. It's motor. I couldn't show my intelligence because I was internally trapped by a motor system that had trouble getting messages from my brain. To be drilled endlessly like I described was psychologically harmful, especially during the circus of supervision when I performed my drills like a trained dog.

The big day came when I was seven when my mom learned to trust her own observations and ignore the ABA geniuses who figured "Touch your nose!" was good enough for me. I have written much about how she realized I could communicate in my first book, *Ido in Autismland*. But let's just say that her determination and decision to fight on, though the experts thought she was nuts, changed my destiny. My father changed it further by insisting my skills had to be independent. And somehow we found Soma

Mukhopadhyay, mom of Tito and inventor of RPM.

To make it clear, the process of learning to motor plan for communication is hard work and requires skilled instruction. Only fools and ideologues believe otherwise. Gradually I learned to type my thoughts independently on a letter board, keyboard or tablet. This means I express my own thoughts and move my own arm without being touched. It does not mean I need to be alone. The presence of a good communication partner helps us to organize our motor systems. It is pretty obvious to those who understand motor system challenges but utterly baffling to experts who deny motor issues and persist in telling people with autism that they don't understand words.

By middle school I was a full time general education student. I was still autistic but I heard normal lectures and I did the same schoolwork as everyone else, earning excellent grades. I had my aide to go with me and with her help I accessed the general education world. In this way I graduated high school with honors, the first, but not the last, autistic student in my middle and high school to do so. I felt like I was an ambassador showing what is the potential of nonspeaking autistic people.

But I suppose my true impact is in advocacy. I have written two books on autism, contributed to others, blogged, delivered speeches and been featured in the media. My goal is to spread the truth. I wrote *Ido in Autismland* in middle school and high school. I had to correct the misconceptions about autism, to explain the symptoms, to speak out. And the book has surpassed my dreams. It is used in university classes, sells throughout the world, has inspired others to communicate and has been translated into several other languages.

I recently published my second book, a novel called *In Two Worlds*. It is a work of fiction based on true life and I hope will reach an audience beyond the autism world. It tells the story of Anthony, a boy with autism who can't talk or show his intelligence. The reader is invited to experience his two worlds, his inner thoughts and sensory experiences, and his outer world of therapies and frustrating misunderstandings. But it is more than that. Anthony learns to communicate at 16 but his professionals don't welcome the change with open arms, to put it mildly. The book invites the reader to get into the experience of living in Autismland.

My mission and projects are still unfolding. The future chapters of my advocacy and educational work yet to be determined. Thanks to communication, I will be the one to choose what they will be.

Reflection Questions:

1. One of the most powerful ways Ido learned to self-advocate was by writing and publishing books. What format or medium would you use to self-advocate or educate others about your experiences?

2. Ido's advocacy focuses on educating others about misperceptions about autistics who have minimal to no speech. What would be your message to the world in your self-advocacy?

5 TITO MUKHOPADHYAY
KEY POINTS IN MY LIFE AND THE
PURPOSE TO FULFILL

Tito Mukhopadhyay
Texas
30 years old

Highlights:

- Critically acclaimed author of six books, including *How Can I Talk if my Lips Don't Move* and *The Mind Tree*
- Featured in the media, including CNN and in the documentary, "A Mother's Courage"

You have a life, it is labeled as autistic as a sort of explanation to your certain traits and you built the purpose to live because you own yourself, your purpose. Your life is long and the purpose will provide a fuel. Your label will not.

You have the tools - your mind, body and most important of all - your imaginations - yes you can go as complicated as you want. So go ahead and imagine some more! Grow a religion if necessary because whatever religions that are out there do not match with those stories you hold within. That's the way you find the purpose.

You may hold a bunch of keys from your life, look for those old locks kept aside that would resist rust and stubborn noncompliance, then remember to open. Looking for the locks; you may wonder where you have placed them. How much past will you dig up?

You see the past like an uprooted tree. How will you know where to begin? There is exactly no beginning—it's all just a continuation and you are submerged in it like a planet submerged in space.

Key points of my life remain just a bunch of keys and I rattle from point to point submerged in the continuity of life trying to find a right sort of lock that folks who describe autism within them or by observation talk about. What's this lock about that I cannot see? Yet there is this bunch of jingling keys that I hold.

A key point of my life may be an absolute darkness that dwells around the space inside whose womb births galaxies of stories, the Milky Ways of ideas and planets full of substances, gaseous shadows, dotted with lights and non-substances like the colors of black, like footsteps on the surface of the moon. I begin with that darkness as a perfect key point of my life.

Darkness may be a good place to begin. It is the nascent womb where everything began including the points of light called stars. Darkness is where light finds a purpose. That's where my stories are born. "Once upon a time there was a story inside the darkness!" Without stories, keys of my life are non-functional.

I desperately need that something called a lock to make the key functional.

To find the right kinds of key points of life, I must first learn how to find them. How do others find key points? Do they smell them out? Am I doing it all wrong searching the depths of stories? Don't tell me that's another topic for research! Researchers maybe the 'absolute truth' in the hierarchy of humanity. How do they manage to know everything? Once upon a time I used to meet autism experts - lots of them around, jeweled with doctorate degrees. Meeting researchers from different parts of the world were definitely key points in my life. They will tell it all - knew everything about the autism inside and outside; knew everything you wanted to know about yourself. A key point of my life was to study a fully developed researcher!

The thought of their data charts and all those page full of proofs are my major matters to ponder. How they shine their glow through the darkness of mankind. I have categorized researchers in three levels:

1. The questioning ones who pretend to extract your brain with questions to fit you into a category. After that they will type something, and hand it for you to keep inside a brown envelope. You hold those numbers, they measured your mind for the next encounter somewhere else.

2. The observing ones who will sit quiet and watch you misbehave. You know you will misbehave and they know you will misbehave. Keep going. Show them what they want! They will get paid to see you misbehave.

3. The ones who will put your head inside machines and pretend to understand the graphs. You know they haven't understood a thing. They know they haven't understood a thing. Never mind that. They are getting paid for that thing they measured. Not you!

Once I had heard my mother tell the school when at the IEP, a someone important from 'an expert level of autism' had complained that I am regularly visiting the Principal's office uninvited and sitting at his swivel - chair: "Why don't you use one of your school district's wonderful autism experts to find a solution to this serious problem? I am just a simple parent!" Mother had suggested back. You want to be a behavioral specialist anymore and solve a complexity? First stop complaining.

I like to hand-write what I learn. And I hand-write frequently, dislike being adorned as 'typer or typist', like the touch of pen on paper. I am a traditional caveman in the era of 'typer-type-autistics.' The touch of pencil on paper is uplifting. I learned to hand write using my muscle memory - once upon a time in a different world called childhood. And I haven't given up on speech! The word 'typer' chains me to the prison of a keyboard. Key point of my life is learning to free myself out of a keyboard.

I am lucky to be published. I had hand written manuscripts to show. There is no point bragging about my earlier writings. One moves on, grows up, views change, writes differently.

I do not like those lime light experiences of public speaking. And facing a crowd is visually fatiguing, auditorily insipid.

But tell me a 'good' sentence and I will hear. I am fond of good sentences. I love old fashioned passages - long sentences meandering like those brain maps inside the skull. Read to me a good poetry and I will hear. And you will be surprised to see me communicate my response. My love for sentences makes me create them.

I enjoy being indoors because those walls begin to breathe inside my head and tell me stories of the world outside. I become the brain inside that skull. Then the rest becomes a story. What else are we doing here in our lives anyway? We are stories that we live. Isn't that the purpose? Create the story with 'good' sentences?

I still hold several keys but locks are uncompromising. Stubborn like that piece of chewing gum below the shoe. Once I tried a chewing gum, swallowed it when the taste was gone wondering why those fruity tastes do not stick to the otherwise sticky gum? Autism sticks better on you. How it sticks and when it sticks is a matter to debate. I honor the sticky moment when autism stuck to my life as a key moment. I can swear by autism. I will keep trying to figure out key moments once I learn how to.

Reflection Questions:
1. Tito explains that without stories the keys to his life are non-functional. Explain the role stories play in your life. Do you create them? Do you share them? What are they like?
2. Tito does not like being adorned with the words typer or typist. He emphasizes that he also writes and speaks. What are your feelings about being called a speller, typer, typist, etc.? What are the advantages and disadvantages to these labels?

CREATIVE AND EMERGING WRITERS

6 SAMEER DAHAR

Sameer Dahar
Ohio
19 years old

Highlights:
- A creative writer who weaves scientific notions into his poetry and essays
- His poems have been transposed into opera performances

I am a gifted teenager with autism. As I am primarily non-speaking, I am a strong advocate for those who have no voice. I use an iPad and letterboards to spell and type for communication. I have spoken about autism in local organizations in the greater Cincinnati area, including The Parent and Professional Autism Workgroup at Children's Hospital, the Islamic Center of Greater Cincinnati, as well as nationally. I participated on a self-advocacy panel at the 2014 and 2015 US Autism Aspergers Association World

Conference as their first non-speaking presenter, sharing my PowerPoint presentation on my life experience with autism.

Despite my challenges, I am successfully pursuing my studies at the Ohio Virtual Academy online school and was inducted into the National Junior Honor Society. My goal is to become an astrophysicist and writer. I am currently typing a book describing my alternative geophysical experience living with autism. My love of science has also led me to study language and autism. I recently presented at the University of Cincinnati's CEES summer program my project entitled "Linguistic Frames in Autism." My writings have also led me down a creative path; my poems "Great Camelot" and "Traversing Great Solitude" have been transformed to opera songs by acclaimed composer Juliana Hall, as part of the Lynx Project, an artistic project pairing art song vocalists and composers with non-speaking writers.

During my homeschool years, I have kept a writing journal. This was an important part of my homeschool curriculum. Desperate for a way to feel heard and my autism understood, I have documented my experiences. The following is one of my entries.

"Life begins in the blackness of space. There, the infinite memory of the cosmos is translated into exothermic force and synthesis of matter. Ontological frames of existence are defined. Knowledge gives birth to action. Long ago my life was devoid of light. I was a black hole, absorbing my surroundings in silence. The patterns of surrounding satellites and gravity locked me into a hopeless dance of collusion. Then mother shined; an intense supernova generating knowledge and understanding. My physical force triumphed over my duplicitous nature. I learned to communicate.

Describing this process of being is difficult. In autism having control is a paradox. Each nerve's locality is perturbed by a quagmire of sensory chaos. Only my thinking is perfected. Many times geophysical stimuli are present which I must analyze, characterize to piece together toward global awareness. Discrete idiopathic thoughts must be held captive to the mind. Housed inside this prison, existence is created. Just as fundamental beauty is found in thermodynamics, my intelligence is quantized and hidden from view. The observations of my mental machinery designate patterns in my environment.

These patterns have an organic nature; I am their student. My nuanced observations have made me a scientist. I self-study physics and do my research at the university library. I investigate particle physics, quantum mechanics, group field theory, and mathematical models, knowing my perception is a quantum event. My goal in life is to become a theoretical physicist. I research in silence and the subjects of study are varied but my autism gives me the ability to make connections. It gives me multiple perspectives. I often notice the equations in the textbooks I read are a language of their own. This language is nonverbal. Every language has discrete algorithms with thresholds to cross. Most people's expression has a creative origin combined with linguistic potentials. Expression in non-vocal autistic individuals is marked by mechanical echolalia, certain repetitive words and behaviors. Society views these demonstrations as subhuman; moreover, therapists discourage such efforts on the part of people to communicate. Our motivations are a biological language of their own.

Even today, I struggle to make conversation. Most of my language I cannot vocalize. Memory holds its interpretation locked. I account for a world of imagery and sound, but my voice cannot do it justice. Governing the kingdom of theoretical internal relationships, I am struggling. Moment by moment words and symbols begin a dialogue in sensory chaos. I find meaning, but at times, my still developing, oxygen deprived brain fails to make sense to me.

I can now determine that the registration of our sensory universe not only defines outward reality but also is limited by our geophysical perspective. Perhaps having autism will help me internalize my observations to a meaningful discussion of my existence. In my autism certain abilities are magnified while others are stunted. However, there is a homogenous character, a self-identity which remains intact. Others are puzzled by this dichotomy. However, my understanding of consciousness is nuanced; I see the mind and body are in reciprocation. each build upon the other and each one marks man's intellect against a tide of quantum particle interactions.

It is a path of determined design. I am an astronaut taking part in this impossible journey to a universe of understanding."

Reflection questions:
1. Sameer infuses a passion of his—science—into his writings about his life experiences. What subject or theme would you apply as a metaphor or analogy to make sense of your life experiences?
2. Sameer goes to a university library to gain access to knowledge about physics. If you do not currently have enough access to the subject of your choice, what steps can you take to gain access to that knowledge?

7 SIDDHARTHA GHOSH

Siddhartha (Sid) Ghosh
Oregon
12 years old

Highlights:
- Identifies as and advocates for people with Down Syndrome, autism, and cerebral palsy
- A young poet

"No such Down Syndrome child has yet lived," said the petty person to my mom. My heart quite broke. To reward professionals yacking about low expectations not only perpetuates grossly negligent, hasty and wrong presumptions, but also severe injustice.

How I experience Down Syndrome: not quite the intellectually retarded roach that you are suspecting. God didn't negate our intellect. She ostensibly took away some of the intelligence of special educators.

Reducing humans to foreign objects having exotic ailments has minimized the huge obligations society has towards disabled kids!

Rationally speaking, my host of wonderful diagnoses would have orchestrated my education such that I would be counting my numbers. Normal rules however reward only normal people. Strong human beings around me put my interests over theirs, asking, teaching, begging the world, thus promising me a highly extraordinary possibility of an equal education.

How have I felt going through extreme gaping holes in my education? Quite livid but mercifully my sweet mother knows how to teach. Opinions of others have not changed her killer will to get me reigning over regular mortals.

Some think that because of my "great" achievements I must have little portions of Down Syndrome! Trisomy has indeed permeated every cell of my bulky frame. To sully your real, challenging accomplishments by minimizing your disability is quite insensitive.

Proudly disabled and smart: not very oxymoronic.

My path through this most rewarding but desperately lonely journey may allow others to find inspiration.

From the quiet Down Syndrome adult to the mellow heavily drugged senior, many languish because poor underdogs don't get respect. Real maps to progress as final destination must have plans such that good stuff lies in wait for mankind regardless of gender or age or arrogant perception of mental quotient.

Many really need other people to add value to their lives. God has a different role for everyone. My role is to show the world what happens when mothers place value in their children's intelligence.

How best to have real change: change that history notes years later with a quiet pride.

To admit past failings is the first step. Make it illegal to not let a child study his or her passions. Please start real change by quietly making it in your home.

"Nothing is how it looks, nothing is a curse." – Myself.

Real roads yet to divide

I wait on the roadside.

Roving vehicles pass me by.
Your never-ending cargo of life.
Should I wait or dodge the bait?
-Sid Ghosh

Reflection Questions:

1. Sid argues that people misunderstand and underestimate the intellectual capacity of individuals with Down Syndrome. In what ways does Sid demonstrate that these assumptions can be misguided?

2. Sid expresses his feelings of frustration through poetry. Create a short poem that expresses the way you are feeling today.

8 EMILY FAITH GRODIN

Emily Faith Grodin
California
27 years old

Highlights:
- Was the first student who types to enroll at Santa Monica College
- Expresses herself through poetry and dance

My name is Emily Grodin and I am an intelligent and passionate autistic woman. At twenty seven years old I am dedicated to my role in helping my community work towards the understanding and acceptance it so rightly deserves. I am an active member of society and I am not so different from every other twenty seven year old you might meet.

Using the power of communication through typing, I create moving and powerful writings in the form of poetry and short stories to welcome readers into my mind. Learning to type was a difficult and tedious process, one that makes writing anything of length seem like a very distant dream. It was not long before I realized how much I desperately needed this outlet. And not just as a way to communicate which, is equally as important, but to truly uncover a part of myself that I waited so long to meet. I was able to write about things that made me elated, or depressed, or even angry. And I have always been invited to write them in a creative form. Writing about my experiences helped to not only share, but also to understand myself and give meaning to my role in the world. There were moments when I could have thrown my iPad across the room, but those times I needed to heal through writing more than ever. Writing quickly became my most trusted personal therapy.

In language that is both raw and insightful I invite my listeners into the life of beauty, wonder and also the challenges of living in the not easily navigated world of life and autism. I choose to write of my experiences, the good, the bad and all in between, in hopes of bringing upon a positive shift in autism, and also to nourish and heal as a writer and human. Dedicated to sharing my words relating to the life of an incredibly difficult and yet all the while amazing journey through alternative needs, I desire change for people going through any experience similar to my own. Most importantly I want other autistic individuals and the people who love them to know that they are not alone. The journey through life is best traveled with meaningful connections to the world and people in it. Without a way to communicate and interact in an intellectual way the ride can be a dark and quiet one.

I have worked long and hard to ensure an independent life but that does not mean I have perfected that yet. Many milestones have been delayed for me but that does not slow me down.

As a young adult, college is something that eventually is discussed. And yet college felt like another dream that was unattainable. I have always thought that a college student was the person who raises their hand at the appropriate time and verbally responds to a professor's questions. I imagined a college student to be very different from me. But several college semesters and a handful of essays later, I can tell you exactly what a college student looks like. We are hard workers and we are opinionated. We discuss and speak our mind. We celebrate the differences between us and join as one during class. We become stressed, and we help each other. And we eat a lot of pizza.

College places a very heavy demand through reading, tests and countless written assignments. But all of the hours truly are worth it when the grades come in. I have felt no greater motivation or accomplishment from receiving high marks on my assignments.

As a college student I have taken opportunity to share my work with the community in poetry readings and presentations.

A great pride of mine is teaming up with a group of poets called the Black Scholars. I have learned through this group the meaning of sharing your work with an audience. While I am one to be anxious in many situations, I have found a great desire to share creatively through several outlets. While I consider myself a poet and writer, I am also a dancer and exploring the world of theater. I have found a confidence and joy on stage that I never knew existed. Whether it is a dance or a poem or handling a prop, I find something very magical in knowing that the audience is there to watch and soak in the happenings under the spotlight.

I have made many goals in my adult life and proudly have met many. A personal goal has always been to be a significant part of society. With a lot of help and constant support, I live a very full and busy life. I have volunteered and I have gone to work. I have used much of my time to learn about and discuss current events in the world. I attend school in hopes of becoming introduced and inspired by new and relevant topics. Everyday I have a renewed urge to be involved and to be heard.

While I consider myself a writer at heart I have made it my personal project to become published in order to share my message on a greater scale.

I have opened up about very personal experiences and events in my life to find the connection between my life and autism and also to help others understand the unique person I am.

In addition to the task that I have accepted in healing the world with typing, I am a daughter, a friend, an advocate, and a lover of good food and travel. I hope that anyone living in silence can find the same light through pushing towards communication. I remind others who are struggling with communication that it is worth the hours of diligent work and practice to be a part of the wonderful life around us.

Reflection questions:
1. At first, Emily did not know that her dream of going to college would eventually become reality. What is a big dream you have that you aren't sure is possible? What are ways you can work toward accomplishing that goal?
2. Emily expresses herself creatively through poetry and dance. What are ways in which you express yourself besides typing and spelling? Are there other ways you hope to express yourself in the future?

9 BENJAMIN LATTANZI
KITE WILL FLY

Benjamin Lattanzi
Florida
19 years old

Highlights:
- His goal is to go to college one day
- He loves to play tennis and surf

A lot of understanding of autistics is understandably wrong. One thing is that too many autistics have to need the help of others. Another thing is that understanding is a tough thing because so many neurotypicals make so much noise. All the noise.

All the noise.

All the noise.

Having to really make yourself listen.

A lot makes you not so good. You have to make yourself happy to please your loved ones. So much to make yourself happy. Because you have to make yourself happy it is maladaptive, too maladaptive to many. A challenging moment is really a lot. Challenging moments include so much time because you live really by yourself. You need a lot of support. A lot of your needs are too hard to make yourself do. You make yourself not need things so you do not ask. Others make us make too many behaviors. They have to ask us too many things.

Laymen born to parents with an education are very advantaged. Because they really see me. Because they make time. Because they see more. Laymen understand a lot about God. About having your God with you and very much having your happiness in loving God. You really have to make your main love in God. You have to pray. It really helps to pray.

Spelling is not making yourself talk but it helps with your happiness. It helps you love yourself. It helps with education. I am happy to spell. I so want to go to college. I'm not sure if I can but I will try.

A lot is really helping yourself so much to make yourself who you will become. Be very mindful to last so long to make a name for yourself. It's really all you've got to really live. Be yourself to make yourself go places and make yourself happy. Fly like a kite.

Kite Will Fly Today

Reflection Questions:
1. Ben explains that independent tasks and skills are difficult when he says, "A lot of your needs are too hard to make yourself do. You make yourself not need things so you do not ask." What sorts of things do you wish to do on your own? When do you feel encouraged to ask for assistance?
2. Ben advises us to be ourselves in order to "go places and make yourself happy" like a kite. If you were a kite, what places would you go? What about these places would make you happy?

10 RISHAN PAVAN

Rishan Pavan
California
9 years old

Highlights:
- Young comedian
- Describes himself as a soldier

How does a typer yell?

By pounding the letter. Now the problem is I can't yell, "Stop talking about me." Also, I cannot pound the letters hard enough to make you believe the words are mine. I am a new typer to this world. You can get to know me by my jokes. I'm funny and I like to make people laugh! You can thank me later for always bringing joy. Before I met my autism brothers I did not see a point in communicating. Really, it is hard and I am a sloth. I see the nice slow pace as good. Now that I have friends just like me I see why I need my words to be heard. They are teaching me I am important and having autism is ok because I am a special gift to this world. I look up to them and they give me hope that I can stop pounding letters to be noticed.

My first happy moment was talking to mom. I learned it is fun to have real good jokes with mom. I love her and being able to talk is really special. My most joy comes from learning real things. I get to do math, science, history, to learn about people and read books. I am most happy to learn my life has purpose. I am being taught that I can do so many things.

I want to be a vampire when I grow up. That was a joke. I just want to be brave. My friends are brave and help me grow. I am not sure I will be a leader but I will make a difference for every person I meet. I am a seriously good looking kid and that is my secret weapon and how I teach people to not look away from autism. I may never be a General but I will always be a soldier.

Reflection Questions:
1. Rishan learned from his friends and "autism brothers" that communication is important, as difficult as it can be. The desire to connect with his friends inspired him to put forth the effort to communicate. What inspires you to communicate?
2. Rishan catches peoples' attention with his humor and good looks. Describe ways that you purposefully catch the attention of people around you.

VISUAL AND PERFORMANCE ARTISTS

11 LARRY BISSONNETTE

Larry Bissonnette
Vermont
62 years old

Highlight:
- Critically acclaimed artist and painter
- Starred in the documentary, "Wretches & Jabberers"

Taking my life as a picture of an autistic man with artistic talent, sophisticated language, problems with behaviors and love of good beer, I would land myself on the platform of keeping people in the community so real progress on communication can happen. I participated on the periphery of social interaction for much of my life. It wasn't until I was given a keyboard and support to use it that I voiced my really important and meaningful ideas.

Many people think its passion for art in my studio that fuels me. But it is realism of needing people's practice of communication support and not having it regularly offered that leads me to place the issue of communication rights prominently on the programmed with Larry sounding professional voices iPad. It's once in another person with autism's lifetime opportunity to move the way society thinks about autism, picking up the pieces of the autism puzzle and repositioning them to highlight the strengths of people instead of looking at their failings which aren't their doing. It is the lack of society to provide opportunities for learning and potential reaching to get to the peak of one's potential as a contributor to their communities and movements for social change.

I once participated and played in my neighborhood's noisy kid's street games at another time in my life. I was a boy without a meaningful way to communicate real thoughts and feelings. Very loving parents did more to make me feel lasting connection to family. Bringing me out in the community was difficult because I only could run around and many people thought I was retarded because I made noises and did odd movements. It wasn't of course retardation but autism that was planting these noises and movements, letting my intelligence stay buried under the surface of behavior. Owning a communication device at that time was probably impossible to conceive of because it looked like a man on the moon idea to position a person like me, pictured by society as not capable of real thoughts and ideas, on the same plane as normally speaking people.

I was the boy lacking practice of more acceptable behavior on the playground and made nothing easy for his parents. Participation in school was not an option so I was sent to live in the state institution for over ten years until I was a young adult when I was able to move into the community into an apartment program. Most of my time there wasn't focused on communication but on learning daily living skills and managing my behavior.

Appearing on the outsider art scene also happened during this time when people in the Vermont art world saw my work and began to put it into exhibitions. Making most of my art on my own, it was totally exciting to see people interested in my art and inspired by my talent. Teaching me how to communicate my thoughts on a computer keyboard came about later after I moved back home with my family in the late nineteen eighties. Easily practicing typing was not my pattern and I had to be pushed to move past my scripted language, hoping that the real words that were in my head would come out into the world so that people could partner autism with intelligence and creativity when they interacted with me. Urgency of looking at my autism as a set of behaviors to be molded into lesser problems of odd social actions was transformed into a path of learning to become a professional movie star and presenter at conferences and workshops.

Others might let me practice leading a life of leisure playing bowling and drinking coffee and craft beer. But people like movie director, Gerry Wurzburg, pushed me to make a movie on the lives of people like me who type to communicate lacking articulate speech but having profound intelligence and perfectly normal knowledge about the world.

The movie was a good look at how people with autism can try new things like sushi and little taxi cabs in a large city. In the middle of doing the film, I started to read my typed communication out loud. Pleased that I could do this, I began to order coffee much more confidently. Placing me in many different situations which required more interaction with people moved me to pull out words into my louder than normal voice and led me into the world of small talk and movie star conversation. This allowed me to work on improving my speech in real life situations.

Lots of my subsequent opportunities to present and show my art have been the result of making this movie and having it been seen by people around the world. It is the partnership of the opportunities to make a difference in attitudes about autism and intelligence with my progress in communication that has propelled me into my life as a popular autism celebrity.

Towards the purpose of educating others about most hard to understand concept of presuming the competence of people without ordered for real intelligent conversation speech, the film has been a perfect learning by observation of real people tool. Would it be progress if people like Tracy Thresher, Larry Bissonnette and other typers of communication sprout up in more documentaries or would it be looked at as pleasing sideshow to move people to a less premade set of assumptions about autistic people? It will soon be known because people like opportunities to watch block busters with music to look at.

Using my intelligence to present meaningful ideas about art, the power of iPadded communication and autism has been the most satisfying accomplishment of my life. People now look at me like a learned person of artistic ability and intellectual capacity who can step out on a stage lit up by iPads and speak about the inclusion and acceptance of people with disabilities. I can now plant myself in the land of People Magazine stories and liked on Facebook postings like any talking star of movies, and that is ok with me.

Reflection Questions:

1. In his narrative, Larry reflects on participating "on the periphery of social interaction for much of my life." What are the moments in which you feel your participation is peripheral (not center stage)? What supports do you need to participate more fully in those situations?

2. Larry is a pioneer in typing to communicate and has been recognized for his art and participation in a documentary. If you were to write an autobiography about yourself, what major events in your life would you highlight?

12 DAMON KIRSEBOM
ON FIRE

Damon Kirsebom
17 years old
British Columbia, Canada

Highlights:
- Award winning painter
- Has achieved independent typing

A fire burns within me. My desire to advocate for autistic individuals who spell or type their thoughts emerged quite naturally, when, at age 15, I learned to independently type out my own thoughts. I regularly communicate with doctors, psychologists, educators and parents about the ways in which non-speaking/non-reliably speaking individuals are misunderstood. Many have remarked that meeting me has shifted their perceptions of non-speaking autism; I always emphasize that I am not a unique case. Recently, I advocated for my future by successfully completing a comprehensive educational assessment. The results, which demonstrated my cognitive capabilities, will allow me to realize my dream of attending university.

I don't just limit my efforts to typing—I find visual ways to advocate. I enjoy painting, and recently exhibited my work. My artwork attracted great attention, and sparked a conversation about being misunderstood, just as I had intended. One of my paintings even won first place in a competition! Currently, I am creating artwork which highlights why spelling and typing are accessible modes of communication for people with sensory-motor differences. Moreover, with a professional artist, I am consulting on a graphic manual which illustrates examples of the lived experiences of someone like me. I hope to demonstrate that outward appearances can be incongruous with thoughts and intentions.

Social media allows me to reach people with whom I might never otherwise interact. I recently shared a video of myself on a website (UCC) which advocates for the right to use one's communication method of choice. I also share my thoughts, interests, activities and accomplishments through Instagram and Facebook. One message I hope to spread is the reality that non-speaking autism is a neurological difference, not necessarily a cognitive deficit.

Perhaps my greatest advocational asset is my genuine desire to connect with people. I am most persuasive when I am true to my self. I ask friendly questions, and relate my experiences with the trust that others will see me as the person I am, rather than the stereotype that is my diagnosis.

One might think, from reading about my life, that my journey has been a smooth one. I assure you, it has not. For so long, I had no means of communication. I was at the mercy of a body that does not cooperate with my intentions (severe apraxia). The words that came out of my mouth were rarely what I was thinking (I talk frantically about hamburgers and fries, and repeat scripts that often have no relevance to the situation at hand). People made inaccurate assumptions about me based on my (uncontrolled) actions, and innocently took me at my (unreliable) word, which led to so much frustration. I had been integrated into general education classes throughout elementary school, and exposed to a rich base of knowledge. When I entered grade eight, however, I was segregated with students who, like me, were considered to be of low cognitive ability. In our class, we worked on life skills such as riding the bus or folding towels, and low-level schoolwork such as first-grade reading or simple addition. It was unbearable; I could feel my life slipping away. Naturally, my parents had tried to reach me. For more than 12 years, I was in a behaviour program which helped me learn motor tasks, such as dressing myself, but did not improve my ability to communicate authentically.

I had just entered grade nine when I learned to express what was in my mind. When an instructor showed me how I could point out letters to spell words, I was overjoyed! Over the next few months, with much hard work, I came to spell quite proficiently. Suddenly, I was able to reframe my future. For the first time in my life, I could ask questions, share my ideas, and be truly known. It was with shock that I learned my special education teacher would not allow me to use a letterboard to spell at school. It nearly broke me.

As I considered the injustice of my situation, a fire began to glow within me. The realization that I could be freed by typing prompted me to urge my mum to help me transition my skills. Within a few desperate and very frantic months, I learned to type, independently, on a keyboard and an iPad on my desk. School administrators, on the advice of my teacher, declined to even see my typing ability. I felt the weight of this attitude like an anchor—one that meant to hold me in place at the bottom of society.

A new school placement, amazing teachers, and a high-level, multi-disciplinary assessment team helped rescue me from my misery. With their willingness to see past my outward presentation, I produced documentation concluding that I am academically capable of working at grade-level, and that my typing is authentic. It is open-minded allies like these that help save people like me. My gratitude and renewed confidence stoked the flames of resistance in me.

My advice to people beginning their spelling journey is this: have high expectations of yourself, and persist through doubt. For me, constantly pushing my skills towards greater independence in communication has paid off—though it's extremely difficult! With each keystroke, I imagine writing myself into the life I deserve. Another important element for me has been engaging in physical activities, which build my ability to control my body's movements. I mountain bike, ice skate, downhill ski and drive an ATV with confidence; and am learning to play ice hockey. The level of real risk increases my mental focus, and forces me to control my movements under challenging conditions. The result is that I have greater movement abilities and greater fortitude in everyday situations.

My inner fire burns brightest when faced with injustice. I have learned through my journey that I am a member of a resilient group—people who are capable of advocating for themselves, and for one another. Non-speaking individuals, after all, should have the opportunity to realize their dreams—just like anyone else!

Reflection Questions:
1. Damon advocates for other individuals who type and spell to communicate through his art, social media posts, and a graphic manual. What kinds of media would you use to advocate for your rights?
2. Because Damon has achieved independence in his typing, he is featured as an advanced communicator on the United for Communication Choice website. Please view his video at https://unitedforcommunicationchoice.org/damon-kirsebom-when-people-see-me-typing/851/. What is your response to his message?

13 ADAM J. MORGAN
MY CHOICE, MY VOICE, MY RIGHT

Adam J. Morgan
Missouri
17 years old

Highlights:
- Has his own YouTube channel called Tech Talk
- First nonspeaking student to take the ACT standardized exam for college entrance in his district

The world I live in can be very lonely, people have opinions about me that are wrong, but because I communicate differently, I don't get to tell them they are wrong about their assumptions. For me, my mom helps others understand my world but it's still very hard. I'm very intelligent, so much that I just do math in my head but can't explain the steps. I have taught myself several other languages but showing people that I know that is near impossible. I read at a high level but if you assess me, I would fail. I'm trapped inside a body that is broken, my only way of showing you who I really am is through my iPad; it is my voice. I feel many people see me as less than a charity case. For they see all the things I can't do, the outbursts or bad behaviors. I very much think others see a very sad future for me. It hurts to go through life knowing that I will always have to fight for everything. Others see autism as a death sentence, but it's not. It's a gift, a superpower. My reality is very different than what others perceive of me; I am smart and just learn and communicate differently. I believe that everyone should be accepted for who they are.

I've always been judged because I don't communicate like others think I should. My parents believe in me and accept me for who I am and how I communicate. When I was in about third grade, age eight, my mom came home from a conference. She had met a young boy, Ido Kedar, with autism that didn't communicate with verbal words but in written word. He showed her what was possible. My mom read his book on the airplane ride home. She finally understood I was in there but that my body doesn't always work with my brain. As soon as my mom got home, she came upstairs to my bedroom and apologized for not believing in me fully. She was very sad and crying. She told me she would doubt me no more—from now on she was going to push me and believe in me. My mom asked me if I could read. I was so happy I tackled her with the biggest hug, I wouldn't let go. I knew from that very moment things would be different. We got to work and bought an iPad and started working with technology. Having my mom and dad on my side means the world to me. This was just the beginning.

I will never forget the moment my life changed forever, the time I first typed my first word. I was ten years old and working with my tutor. She believed in me so she got out my iPad and gave me my first learning opportunity to share my own thoughts instead of making a choice. Her approach to me was so caring and full of hope so much that I wanted to make her proud. I spelled with her for the first time, it was amazing.

I communicate by typing with support. I have to have a constant connection through touch in order for my body to connect with my brain to get my thoughts out. I must have a communication partner that believes in me and how I communicate. How it looks is just different, not wrong. When people think it's my partner typing for me, it hurts. For those that don't believe, I hurt for you because you are missing out on a learning opportunity to change the stigma of people who learn and communicate differently. How someone communicates is not going to impact you directly, it is my right under the law to choose my preferred communication method not anyone else, only me. Be open-minded, not judgmental, it doesn't just give you a different perspective it makes you a better person.

Middle school was my toughest years. I was treated like a baby and everyone had low expectations. I hated it so much I'd get out of the car and sit on the curb and cry. The staff took that as I didn't know where the door was but in reality, I hated going to school and how they treated me. My parents moved me to a better school and things were much better, but they still wouldn't support my typing. Not everyone understands or accepts the way I communicate. It's still very hard when people don't believe its me typing but I'm getting better at not caring what others think.

I'm a Junior in high school now and not only do my parents believe in me but so do my teachers. I take all general education classes and am getting great grades. I'm on track to get my high school diploma in 2020 with my class and will be headed to college to study mass communications so that I can become a motivational speaker and author to help others follow their dreams. I just found out I'll be the first non-speaking student to take the ACT in my school district and it will be on World Autism Awareness Day.

I have recently started CrossFit and it is great. It makes my body more under control. My lower body is so stiff and the exercises help loosen me up. CrossFit is helping me get my body to follow directions that it doesn't want to follow. My favorite activity is the farmers carry; it helps me stretch and get sensory input in my joints. My trainer is awesome, she treats me like an adult and pushes me. I hope I'm making her proud

The most important thing to know about autism is that it's nothing more than a label. Just remember, the real experts are those of us that live with autism. Just ask us, we will educate you. I've started my own YouTube Channel called Tech Talk With Adam Morgan - https://www.youtube.com/channel/UCBhsakJ4qPCFhhjyPpdkQwA.

Adam J. Morgan – High School Junior

Reflection Questions:
1. Reading Ido Kedar's book was a turning point for Adam and his family. Which book or article has inspired you to think differently about autism?
2. Adam does CrossFit exercises to help him strengthen his motor abilities. What activities or exercises help you feel more in control of your motor movements?

14 JEREMY SICILE-KIRA
MY LIFE WITH COLORS

Jeremy Sicile-Kira
California
30 years old

Highlights:
- Critically acclaimed artist (visit https://www.jeremysvision.com/)
- Co-authored the book *A Full Life with Autism* (St. Martin's Griffin, 2012)
- Representative and advisor to major national autistic initiatives

I like to think like a great teacher once told me: you are the product of your parents and a product of your environment and the reaction you have to both. If you are a hard worker and have great parents and a good school, you will be successful.

Getting out of the darkness for me was not a miracle. It was a team effort of lots of work over a long period of time. My mother found a way for me to learn to communicate using the Rapid Prompting Method (RPM). Greatly the letter-board is my voice. The real reason for my success in life is frankly that my mom got good people to work with me and professionals that believed in me. My success as a person with abilities did not start in high school or college. My success is due to the many years of learning and trying to understand what the world is made of. Gradually over the years I learned to make sense of all things around me.

Despite not being able to speak very much, I graduated from Torrey Pines high school in June 2010 with a full academic diploma, and gave a commencement speech using voice output technology. You can see it on my website: https://www.jeremysvision.com/media.

After graduating from high school, I attended community college part-time. Advocacy for others like me who have no voice is an important part of my life, so I co-authored a book *A Full Life with Autism* (Macmillan 2012) and served as a Youth Representative to the United Nations for the Autism Research Institute (NGO); as a youth leader for the Autistic Global Initiative, and as a youth advisor to the California Employment Consortium for Youth (CECY).

About 6 years ago I began to communicate to my mom and support staff the dreams I was having every night: dreams that I was painting colorful abstract portraits of people I had met during the day. The dreams showed the emotions and personalities of the persons in different colors. Then one night I dreamt I had a great art show of my paintings. Truly I was really excited and asked my mom how I could truly make my dream come true and have an art show.

Mom frankly told me it could not very much happen unless I painted in real life. Truly I was surprised to see I could, by kindly trying hard, to learn to paint. Frankly when I discovered I could in real life paint my dreams, I became a full-time artist. I had my first curated, solo art show (https://www.jeremysvision.com/media) which was covered by local and national media. It lasted two weeks, and was a sold out show, and I also had 24 private commissions.

Now, I am a successful artist. I have an art studio in an art co-op. I live in an apartment with 24 hour supports. Truly I am grateful for my communication partners.

Art has frankly given a meaning to my life. I have a gift called synesthesia. Synesthesia means that the neural pathways relating to senses are mixed creating stimulation of another sense. For example, when I look at a person, I see people's emotions translated into color, and I keenly see great colors in people's faces depending on their mood. The great colors also tell me the type of person they are in regards to their lifestyle choices. I truly do not see the facial movements that show emotions on people's dear faces because I have vision processing challenges. A person's voice elicits colors as well, as greatly does listening to music. Now as an artist I can write a description of what I see, and then I paint the painting.

For commissioned paintings, I meet the client at my art studio, or via Skype or Facetime, and listen to them and watch them. When I dream, I am processing what I have seen and heard when I am awake. Then, in my art studio, I greatly paint the painting from my dream, and use my communication skills to write a description of what I see. Truly I paint vibrant paintings of people's positive energies and emotions, because I believe that if I paint the best in people they will see how beautiful they are on the inside and greatly it will inspire them to act as nicely beautiful human beings. I frankly hope my paintings inspire only the good in people, and I greatly hope that I make a difference in the world with my art.

Frankly I also provide "ability awareness" talks at elementary schools in the San Diego area. First, I visit the school and I hear from or observe some teachers and students. Then I return two months later to give my talk, and presenting the school with a painting of their colors.

Greatly the paintings and description are hung in the school lobby, a daily visual reminder to students and educators to "Believe in yourself," and to "Follow your dreams."

Dearly my gift of being able to paint people's colors is how I feel connected to other people, and can give back to the world. Frankly communication is important to me because it's only through the letterboard or iPad that I can truly be heard, and share my gift of the meanings of each person's true colors. This is how I help others. Frankly you can see examples of my paintings and descriptions on my website.

Imagine what gifts other people who are not given the opportunity to type may have. Without a way to successfully communicate, these gifts may stay hidden forever. Frankly everyone should have a voice.

Kindly I hope my story inspires others. Greatly I hope that after reading about me, you will be inspired to realize that you can make a difference in the world around you, no matter the challenges you face.

Reflection Questions:
1. Jeremy experiences synesthesia by seeing people's different emotions and expressions as different colors. He applies this gift to his art. Name a gift you have. In what way do you apply this gift to a passion, hobby, or activity you enjoy?
2. Imagine that, like Jeremy, you also see particular colors for particular emotions and energy. Describe which colors you would assign or attribute to different kinds of emotions.

15 ADAM WOLFOND
COLLABORATION HAPPENS BY
MANAGING MOVEMENT TOGETHER

Adam Wolfond
Ontario, Canada
17 years old

Highlights:

- Co-founder of The A Collective, a learning community of neurodivergent people
- Conference speaker, film maker, and poet
- Featured in ReelAbilities in Toronto, Canada

I am an artist and poet. I go to high school and am a co-founder of The A Collective. It is a learning community thinking of how to be creative with neurodivergent people. I have made several films and will exhibit at York University Neurodiversity in Relation. I give presentations at universities and conferences and my film was featured at the ReelAbilities Film Festival in Toronto, Canada.

I am non-speaking but have some words and phrases to communicate. I learned to type when I was young and am today, seventeen. My mom has trained a lot of people to support me. I think a lot about language and I want people to understand how hard it is to always type and how I want to express myself also through movement, wanting to talk less. In this essay, I want to talk about how others can understand feeling and movement as a way of communication.

People are mostly focused on speech and smooth body movements as proper way of communication. This is not always my way of language although language is all I am. My language forges like water. Water is open and always moving. When typing I am like a kite taking flight. I need lots of co-pilots to help me land to communicate. Support touches my back or sits beside me and I can initiate my own movements to type. With practice I can also type now on my own because I have arranged the pattern of movement over time. But I want to say that pace and pattern of movement towards typing is important. My supporters allow me to assemble the pattern of movement I need to type my thoughts.

The management of language is making sentences that manage to amaze me and I am eager to race but using the good keyboard I am weaving a lot of thinking and moving into one line at a time. A braid is a brilliant way to see it and I am thinking that all the lines are backing the other ones. Having the ability to think around things and not talk about them clearly amazes language talkers and I am thinking the good writing can do with movement.

Being able to move is important for me to feel space and my body. I use sticks and tap toys to feel my way through the sometimes difficult moving space and the pace of talkers. Communication is also feeling. Feeling is a way of dancing in the space so I can assemble words with my amazing moving body. The way of writing language is like taking a breath.

But movement doesn't always assemble the way of the talkers. Please do not read my movements as dis-ordered.

Ticcing is like an arrangement of my always-moving body. I tic using toys of tall ideas to tap my way through space of the outside world and I sometimes game the space like a backward spiral that tries to find its way.

I sometimes want to be settled and sometimes I want to be moving and I tic because I want to be settled and I tap to feel the way the comings of space arrange me like a forge inside my eyes. I want the amazing arrangement to settle down so I tap to control the amass inside my eyes. I am using the sound of tapping to think and pace like talking.

I really want to easily talk but since I can't I will talk about the tall idea of the way I tap. I am feeling all the time and I am the toy-talker who is always toy-touching to control the forging environment that is always touching me. I am the tapped toy who is always talked at and I am wanting say in how I am touched. Support understands how the assembly of ticcing is like talking and how I language movement.

I communicate in movement. There are many rhythms to think about and I am always split between my open feelings and the way people want me to be pleasing them. It is awful to have to pace myself like others; the tough pacing of having to speak and always move so fast. Ticcing is the way I answer pace. Ticcing is the arrangement of a constantly moving body. People want me to master one way of language but I navigate my movements like a masterful ticcer.

Liking me is about the way talking people are asking me to write mostly about autism and not about dominating language of talkers. Language wants landings. Language wants answers about autism. I want to sometimes be free of words. I want to move and I am thinking about collaboration in art, poetry and movement and not just typing to answer questions. My art thinks about movement to give people ideas of how I don't answer in words.

Pace is important to understand from people who want to know me. I think about movement and time. Think about the way the rocks and the water of the ocean communicate: rocks want the water to talk to them about the language of time. Water talks by pacing waves against them. Rocks respond by having worn surfaces. Time is perceived by the appreciation of language but I am the pace of my body and not language. My body is pacing the task of the feeling of my body, and the feeling of the pace of the environment. I am feeling a lot of things and it's hard to have concentration when I am not able to be at the talking table but in the feelings of the world.

Activating movement happens with the support of another body. There are many different bodies always moving. Support understands how collaboration happens by managing movement together.

Reflection Questions:
1. Adam is a creative writer who uses metaphors, like the ocean and flying a kite, to represent his communication. What metaphor can you think of to describe the dynamics of your communication?
2. Adam explains the joys and challenges of his "always-moving body." What joys and challenges do you experience with regard to movement or motor planning?

FEATURED IN FILMS
AND DOCUMENTARIES

16 DILLAN BARMACHE

Dillan Barmache
California
19 years old

Highlights:
- Featured in a short film by Apple viewed by millions
- University student majoring in psychology and runs on the cross country team
- National conference speaker

Learning to type and spell gave me the opportunity to look into a possible kind of future that I could never have had without intensive support to handle feeling lost in being autistic. Cases like mine are familiar to many of you. It starts hardly pleasant at all. Parents feel there is some hope, so long as they follow the prescribed paths, but those paths offer no voice to the nonspeaking autistic community. I was on those paths for many years until I discovered there was a possibility for more. I found needed supports that were outside the box that allowed me to put my fast-moving thoughts around an anchor. Only then would they come out through my hands to form a single word, then another, and so on until I was truly heard for the first time.

In the early days of training, forces were at battle—autism versus getting focused. You might as well be trying to tame a wild bear. These early sessions kept me hopeful that one day I could say all I was thinking. Outside a middle school classroom at a picnic table, the practice of thinking and moving my finger to the exact letter I needed had begun. It was hardly a proper place, but really was good to feel the support of another person's soul. Deb was a person with a tireless confidence in me. No matter what I did or didn't do, she would never stop believing I was in there; trying to have all the control I knew it would take to fully communicate.

Then flash forward many months, and I am sitting in a general education class trying to keep my autism at bay. For me, these early days were the scariest. I was always scared of the possibility that my journey would end before I could break into the world of true communication. The more I learned to make my mind and body work together to express deeply hidden thoughts, the more I realized that I was gaining something that could be taken away from me. All it would take was a single principal to decide my fate based on outmoded beliefs about autistic students like me, a single teacher to deny my authorship of words, or even simply for my needed support person to drift away. I was gaining freedom through words, but that freedom was like a floating bubble, ready to pop at the slightest touch.

Obstacles did surface. I was in between the worlds of communication and autistic impulse that caused many people to doubt my words were true. When you are a person with such obvious autism and no spoken words coming from your own mouth, you must constantly prove yourself.

There are people who have always and will always yell out to the world that every word I type is not really me. They will say that I am being led by my support person. Those people do not want me in classes of real value. They want me in a room where I will learn to count to ten until I am old enough that I can no longer be in school. Everything I do is evidence that is examined to prove or disprove their assumptions of an empty mind. When I type, they watch to see if it is really me. When I am caught in an autistic cyclone of repeated motions that make no sense, it is evidence that I have no ability to overcome the overwhelming disability that consumes me. I must be aware of the scrutiny that will always come from doubtful minds seeking to denounce me. It is another hurdle on the track of my life and I have leapt over it many times to become the student I am today. I broke free from the prison of silence, and I achieved a valued education in middle school and high school.

By fighting through the doubts of others I was able to learn not just to type my thoughts, but to live out other joys. I joined the cross country and track teams in high school which helped me to become an athlete. I love to run and I still continue to outpace my own anxieties on the trail. It is another kind of freedom I enjoy because of the belief I have in myself and the support of my family. I have spoken at many conferences and events about my experience in front of audiences and even had a short film released by Apple about how I type to communicate. These are not bragging points, they are a window into what is possible for every single autistic person out there in the world who gains the needed support to explore their own lives like I have. Each accomplishment was something that took great hard work and dedication to achieve.

There are moments where autism still sweeps me away with such powerful fury that it is easy to think that maybe I am never going to reach beyond my autism. However, the support of my family and the support I receive from the people helping me to communicate keeps me moving forward to show that I can do many great things.

Now I sit in college classes and I write essays on legal theory and the social justice of land use in Los Angeles. I will not stop because a person without the open mind and heart to hear my voice does not believe I can be doing these things. That is the message that is most important for other educators and professionals to know. When you encounter a student that does not have a voice and you refuse to believe in their intact mind, you have only told them to stop moving forward. You have told them to stay in their world of autism and seek no way out. My message for the autistic community is to ignore those people who stop you. You must always strive to take another step forward because if you stop, you are giving up the joy of your own life. Those who will stop you are not the people who will live your life. The person who will exist every day in a cage built of silence and rote motions and endlessly simple lessons is you. Step forward and fight for your own existence. Those are the lessons I learned by winding through my path to communication and true education.

Reflection Questions:
1. Dillan explained that the "more I learned to make my mind and body work together to express deeply hidden thoughts, the more I realized that I was gaining something that could be taken away from me." What have you earned or worked hard for that you were afraid would be taken away? What can you tell yourself to keep pushing forward in spite of this fear? What supports or resources can you tap into when there is a threat of losing what you have worked for?
2. Dillan's compelling message to teachers is that "when you encounter a student that does not have a voice and you refuse to believe in their intact mind, you have only told them to stop moving forward." What major piece of advice would you give to teachers to help them become better instructors to autistic students?

17 PEYTON GODDARD

Peyton Goddard
California
44 years old

Highlights:
- Featured in two documentaries, "Helium Hearts" and "Restraint and Seclusion: Hear our Stories"
- Author of memoir, *i am intelligent*
- Progressed from years in segregated schools to becoming the valedictorian of her community college

I live to teach "Treasure all - great is each." I advocate valuing all people, especially those most vulnerable to devaluation, segregation and abuse, as I was for decades when I lacked a dependable mode of communication.

I was born a joyous child wired differently. I can appear to move well, but ultimately intentional movement is hard for me. I experience freezing paralysis of getting stuck or motor madness of repetitive actions I cannot stop without sweet understanding support. I'm not trusty-powered by my ordering my own neurons; I live scared that I cannot move my body as my mind requests, generating almost constant red fears I will fail and lose yet another opportunity for a real life.

Early intervention testings and therapies began, increasingly with the goal of curing my differences. Many deficits were measured, and limiting labels layered on…severely mentally retarded, low-functioning autistic, etc. With no way to tell I'm competent, I'm treated as throw-away trash and deemed unfit for public schools. Despite my parents' efforts to support me, I suffered years of neglect and abuse in institutions where, due to my unpredictable body, I was considered incapable of learning. In years of private placements, wherever I was judged un-intelligent, non-compliant or inappropriate, aversive interventions permeated my being. Each time I'm appearing to them not trying to do my best. Instead of so-called "educators" hearing I need their help, I'm locked away in hidden rooms that pointed loudly "I'm worthless." I wanted to tell the agony, but I could not. I'm traumatized. I'm sad. I years tried telling myself sweet lies that the tortures did not matter. But with each looming locking, part of me is pity-killed. Locks re-torture. No certain child should greet locks.

By age sixteen, I was deeply depressed. Medicines offered no help. Pills could not heal my tumbling, gyred, sorrow-filled, terrorized soul. Bitten by the beast of separation, resolved I became to never being included in the real world. My yells for a just peace wallowed. Segregation denied me reaping a potent education. Accommodations and true support were absent. Segregation denied me desired friendships. Joy was a word lost. Hope I filed as a barren cause. Wisps of doubt that things would ever change were quoted in my teasing life.

My parents pulled me out of restrictive placement, and tastes of inclusion brought tiny glimmers of hope. However, my uncooperative body continued to hinder my ability to communicate and participate until, at age 22, I was supported to type. In my first typing session, when asked what I would like to say, I typed "i am intlgent." I finally gained a mode of dependable communication, which allowed me to tell the truth of my life and begin to relieve the fear which plagued me. For that, I each dawn answer, "Thank God." My youth was ruptured, and tears fell that others could not read. Healing is mightily hard but communication makes it possible. Each day I choose to try to heal....so I can help.

"I want a real education" became my urgent plea. At Cuyamaca Community College I found support in ordinary-never professors. They each peered at me with pure helium hearts. They each trod where most journeying educators moll impossible passage. They each opted to reason with my eerie appearances not as pretenses for re-returning me easily to segregation. They each opened their ready measurements, wearing possibility not limits. They each plotted appropriate, treason-never accommodations. Increasingly peaceful I became in the perusal of all learning treats, reaping years of finally actioning real rational, typical thoughts. Four years later in 2002, I became the first person using supported typing to graduate valedictorian from a U.S. college. In 2003, my dad and I produced a video of my life entitled "Helium Hearts." The following year at CalTASH, I was awarded the Mary Falvey Outstanding Young Person Award, which "annually goes to a young person who has demonstrated the values of Cal-TASH through their service or participation in activities promoting inclusion for all people." Because I saw a life I'll never want anyone to teach as acceptable for any human being, I wrote my story. Nothings need to be heard. In 2012, my memoir, *i am intelligent*, was published. My bloody-beared truths are for telling this worrisome world that yearns are in all persons to be verifiably valued and supported by their sisters and brothers. There is vast value in all humans. We are all better together. In 2013, I shared my story in the film "Restraint and Seclusion: Hear our Stories" by Dan Habib, filmmaker at the Institute on Disability at the University of New Hampshire.

I live with support in my own apartment and continue to present at conferences, at universities to future educators and speech pathologists, to community organizations and parent conferences. I'm progressing on my quest to speak intentionally. For the last 4 years I have been collaborating again with Carol Cujec, PhD. on our middle-school age ('tween years up) novel REAL about inclusion, featuring a non-speaking, neuro-diverse protagonist who types to talk, based on my life.

My advocacy is centered on teaching that pertinence for all is the way to peace for all. Children and parents long to know that different is both ok and welcomed. Difference is in all of us. Fear it we do not need. We are one in unity of creation. Segregation bites us all. Sadder we both are separated than togethered. It is wepted ignorance of each other that will cheat us all. In the awe of together lie golden poignant possibilities. Including and supporting diverse persons to have lives of real opportunities heals fears of imperfections in all of us. Peace will come when all persons matter to the whole.

Reflection Questions:
1. Peyton made the incredible leap from being segregated for years in restrictive school placements to enrolling in a community college and becoming valedictorian. What do you believe are the qualities and attitude that Peyton needed to achieve this feat?
2. Peyton is co-authoring a novel about "inclusion featuring a non-speaking, neuro-diverse protagonist who types to talk, based on my life." If you were to write a novel, what would it be about? Describe the protagonist.

18 MATT HAYES

Matt Hayes
Missouri
21 years old

Highlights:
- Star of Emmy winning PBS documentary "My Voice: One Man's Journey to Overcome the Silence of Autism"
- National conference speaker
- Poet

In my grand ideas of life, I see myself doing many things that people would say are impossible. That may be true, but if my starting line is doubting myself, I will never begin the race. My mom once said to me, "You will talk." I believed her. My voice is stilted, and my spoken words need written letters to help me speak, but every day I can feel my impossible-to-unlock voice grow stronger.

I want to drive a car. I want to get married. I want to have a good paying job. I want kids to love. These seem like impossible dreams, but once upon a time I couldn't ride a bike. I dreamed of flying down the road on two wheels with wind whooshing through my hair, careening around corners, mastering the road with speed. I hoped and dreamed and waited and worked, mastering one small piece at a time. It was excruciatingly hard and slow but so rewarding to learn those micro steps. Finally, I learned to balance. I was flying now. In dreams and reality, bike wheels were my wings. It took many mini steps to ride my own bike. Now I ride twenty miles and feel like an overcomer.

My hope is that what we fear is not what we focus on. We lose nothing by pursuing what we truly want. It is only in our fear that we are caged.

I was very young when I started riding horses with sidewalkers in hippotherapy. I wanted very much to ride on my own, but I needed someone with the patience, courage, and skill to help me get there. Most of all I needed someone who believed I could learn. I was not expecting to ride without sidewalkers when I went to Valley Mount Ranch for lessons, but Sheila who ran the ranch looked at me and said, "He can learn to ride, and I want to teach him." I wanted to ride independently, but this was scary. By her voice, I knew Sheila meant it. We were going to do it, and I had better hold on tight. Hold on tight was just what I did. Sheila took me round and around the arena, through hills and bluffs, across creeks and bridges, in meadows and woods. She took off the lead rope and boxed me between horses in front and back on the trail. She found a horse that understood me and became my very own. We walked and trotted in heat and cold.

After all of it, Sheila gave me a job at the ranch. It was hard work, and I loved it. I would walk through fire for any of the ranch crew and especially Sheila because they believed in me and treated me like one of them. Now I believe that I can do anything if someone first believes enough to give me a chance.

I have had many incredible opportunities, but these accomplishments built something in me that I carry to everything else that I try and achieve.

Trusting yourself takes courage. There is nothing my heart has wanted that didn't involve overcoming my own fears.

I was afraid to write my first poem and openly share it until a friend said, "Matt, write a poem." I was terrified to write more poems, thinking they wouldn't be as good as my first. I was both terrified and excited to meet other poets because I felt young, inexperienced, and unworthy, but those experienced poets helped me find my poetry voice. They reached out through the autism to hear my words, encourage those words, and help prune what wasn't working in the poems without crushing my spirit. They believed in me and gave me a chance.

Every fear we overcome is a stepping stone to freedom. The people we long to know may be the ones who lend a hand to pull us up as we step higher on wobbly legs.

Living is an adventure if we let it be. We watch and read adventure stories forgetting that those heroes are often afraid as well. They are heroes because they take the step that is before them.

Our travels as autists are not easy. Our climb is steep and long, but we have creative minds and deep, enduring loyalty, and these are massive strengths. The willingness to share who we are is our key responsibility. Often when we finally get communication, many of us have been silent for so long we are unsure how to climb out of our cage and reveal our true selves.

As someone who has used typed communication since childhood, I have had a long time to practice putting my thoughts into words. It is a skill that takes time and practice. I want to communicate like I think, but it doesn't work like that. The translation process of thoughts to words must occur. It takes commitment to increase communication and facilitate friendships that go beyond question and answer. To be a friend, I must translate my deeper thoughts into words and willingly share essential pieces of myself. In these deeper friendships real life takes place. This journey demands connection for us to be our best. We are not going very far if we remain undiscovered islands.

I have been given many incredible opportunities: the Emmy winning PBS documentary "My Voice: One Man's Journey to Overcome the Silence of Autism," my book with co-author Thalia Pryor, my poetry mentors, and opportunities to speak at conferences, but in each instance I am indebted to friends who saw a spark that they helped fan into a flame.

I would give friends this advice.

Be a friend.

Be authentically yourself.

Trust even when you are afraid.

Remember no one ever succeeded all on their own.

Thank the people who help you by truly caring about them.

Give yourself time to reach your goals.

Express what it is you really want and believe you will get there one step at a time.

Research Questions:

1. A theme that permeates Matt's narrative is fear. Fear of things like being "inexperienced and unworthy" and "revealing our true selves." Matt reminds us that heroes also experience fear. What fear do you experience? What helps you overcome this fear?

2. In Matt's advice at the end of his narrative, he urges you to realize your goals one step at a time. Name one major goal you hope to accomplish. Describe the steps you need to take to get there. Use this as an action plan for yourself.

19 SUE RUBIN

Sue Rubin
California
41 years old

Highlights:
- The focus of "Autism is a World," an Academy Award nominated documentary
- National award-winning advocate
- Graduated with a bachelor's degree from Whittier College

For the first thirteen years of my life, I actually lived the typical life of a non-verbal autistic person who was assumed to be intellectually disabled. I was diagnosed shortly after birth with developmental delay, which turned into a diagnosis of mental retardation, now "intellectual disability." At four I was also diagnosed with autism. From stimming to Special Day classes, to full inclusion, to carrying the Olympic torch, to graduating from high school with honors, to being accepted to Whittier College, to a Bachelor's degree, to a consulting business, has been an amazingly awesome journey.

My special education years were state of the art with integration with regular education students and real life experiences in the community. I had lots of speech therapy, but apraxia stopped me from speaking. So we tried pictures, which didn't work well either since any kind of purposeful movement was impossible for me. I also suffered from behaviors often seen in autism such as biting, yelling, scratching, and head banging.

Life changed drastically when in the eighth grade I was introduced to facilitated communication (FC) by my speech therapist and educational psychologist. We were trying to replicate what the psychologist had seen with a non-verbal autistic young man who was really violent and who everyone thought was intellectually disabled. This young man was able to type answers to questions the facilitator could not have known. When I attempted typing, I was able to spell my name and find some letters in some words. We contacted Syracuse University to learn more about FC. My mom and the speech therapist eventually became leaders in the field. When we started we had a facilitator push back at my hand, then gradually reduced the support until I could type without physical support.

Shortly after our first attempt at FC, my mom asked in an I.E.P. that I be taught how to read. The Severely Handicapped teacher hadn't been taught how to teach reading since we were not supposed to be able to learn to read. So the teacher asked her sister who was a Learning Handicapped teacher. They decided to teach me phonics. The next week the speech therapist called my mom and told her to forget phonics. She asked the class what we do with our families and I spelled "vacation" correctly. I guess I was actually learning all those years I was going into regular education classes. My teacher gave me a standardized arithmetic test and I was able to do simple addition, subtraction and some multiplication and division. I may have learned it when my brother, two years older than me, was using flash cards whenever we went on road trips. My mom taught me fractions and long division in an afternoon.

I believe my mind was disorganized. My mom was having me read high interest, low vocabulary books but I was not understanding them for several months. It seems that the more I typed, the more organized my brain became. Words no longer floated over my head but became meaningful, the stories began to make sense, and I became aware of the world around me. By spring of the eighth grade I was attending some regular education classes and was expected to do homework.

Over all my high school experience was awesome, allowing me to excel. After I won a contest writing about Cesar Chavez, we sent it to the Los Angeles Times, which resulted in me being awarded a United Farm Workers flag at an assembly where all the students stood up to honor me. At Whittier high I met life-long friends and was even a bride's maid for a friend who worked for me as a staff person after we graduated. In spite of my awful autistic behaviors I was able to graduate with honors and was accepted to Whittier College with a $38,000 academic scholarship. Professors actually liked me being in their classes and were extremely patient and accepting. After sixteen years I graduated as a member of Phi Alpha Theta, International Honor Society in History, with a Bachelor's degree in Latin American History. That day was amazing with first the faculty then everyone in the audience standing, yelling, and applauding me. Without having been included in regular education in high school, I never could have attended college, which was an amazing experience intellectually and socially. The highlight, besides graduation day, was when I went to Cuba with my Latin American music class. I have found that when I am intellectually active my awful autistic behaviors are reduced. I must keep busy or autism swallows me.

I have received many honors since I began typing to communicate: Woman of the Year in Education, presented by State Senator Tony Mendoza; the Baron Inspirational Award, Julia Ann Singer Center; the Supported Life Institute, the Autism Society of America, and CALTASH. An exciting day for me was when I carried the Olympic Torch in 1996 with the help of a more coordinated friend who would not set L.A. on fire. Perhaps the most exciting event in my life was when Autism is a World, a documentary about my life with autism, was nominated for an Academy Award and I got to go to Oscar night. We were picked up in a limousine, driven to the Kodak theater, and walked the red carpet in front Johnny Depp and behind Gwyneth Paltrow. When we walked in people recognized me and wished me luck.

I also have written several articles myself and have had several articles written about me in publications such as Newsweek, and Disability and Society. I have been featured on KCET and in DVDs about autism. And I have written chapters in three books: *Education for All: Critical Issues in the Education of Children and Youth with Disabilities, Autism and the Myth of the Person Alone*, and *Sharing Our Wisdom*.

As a self employed autistic consultant, I am able to offer advice to families and other autistic people so they too can be as successful as I have been. Please see my website: sue-rubin.com

Reflection Questions:
1. Sue Rubin was one of the first nonspeaking students to graduate from college in the United States, paving the way for other students who type and spell to communicate to go to college. In what ways do you hope to pave the way for future generations of autistic and disabled individuals?
2. Sue attended the Oscar's and walked the red carpet when the documentary about her life with autism was nominated for an Academy Award. In your wildest dreams, what award would you like to win one day and for what accomplishments?

20 TRACY THRESHER
THE COMMUNICATION CONNECTION: LIVING A LIFE OF PURPOSE

Tracy Thresher
Vermont
52 years old

Highlights:
- Starred in the documentary, "Wretches and Jabberers"
- A pioneer and advocate in using facilitated communication
- Has become an award-winning Master Trainer in facilitated communication

My name is Tracy Thresher and I have been using facilitated communication for over 25 years now. I want people to know me as ferocious Tracy and I will yell about my right to communicate. I was one of the first people to start using facilitated communication in Vermont and it allowed me to let people know how intelligent I am. It is hard for me to communicate in any other mode, my speech is very unreliable and to really access my thoughts I need to type. With the right support I am able to say the words I want to say.

I am the autistic man. The one who big time would like you to know that movement is my disability. With my body taking over into "auto-mode," my brain shuts down. For example, I walk daily letting my body do its thing, but my brain sleeps and I lose track of where I am, sometimes having covered long distances! Perhaps I look like I don't understand these things but I do. What's hard is for me to show you.

The introduction to typing was very much needed and without it I am sure I would have fallen into despair. It was truly a life changing moment for me. I have always felt lost in autism and ironically my journey started when my mom first received the diagnosis. It became a sentence to a life of obstacles and in my early years I was angry and cursed God for making me this way.

I have lived in Vermont all of my life. I was in special education for all of my school years; my teachers did not understand my needs and relied on my verbal communication mostly. It was not my most reliable form of communication so at times I also used my behavior. I know that actions speak louder than words but no one knew how intelligent I was; I was smart but had no way to express myself. I desperately needed a more reliable way to communicate.

I was introduced to facilitated communication in the early nineties and I will be forever grateful to Bill Ashe and Alan Kurtz who knew there was intelligence behind my often purposeful behavior. Since expressing my voice through typing I have changed dramatically in the way I view the world. I have pursued my dreams with unrelenting ferocity to the point where I am amazed to see the evolution of my inner thoughts. Becoming the positive thinking man I dreamt to be, rather than the caged beast who could not control the frustration of miscommunication.

It all started long ago when I met Harvey Lavoy in the early nineties. He wanted to hear my plans for the future. I told him I wanted to tell my story to help other people who had communication challenges. Harvey had the idea of advocacy which I hadn't thought of before. I liked the idea but needed direction from others who were doing this type of work. I began networking to meet other self-advocates and connected with Green Mountain Self-Advocates—our statewide self-advocacy network in Vermont—and I worked on projects like changing our services to be more personalized based on individual goals.

I think sitting on committees and other structures that plan for and make decisions about the lives of people with disabilities is extremely important—with so much at stake we need to voice our opinions front and center so that typing is seen as valuable input. It is important to me that I use my voice. Self-advocacy has changed the way I see myself. It is like looking in the mirror for the first time. I like myself better now. It feels better to know I might look intelligent to the world.

In 2009, I completed a Travel-the-World-Tour film project with Harvey, Pascal Cheng, and Larry Bissonette. That was the most awesome experience I have had; going to Sri Lanka, Japan, and Finland. What potential for sensory overload, anxiety, and meltdowns. Not so though, I had more relaxed time than any time in my life. This is what I wanted to do more than anything in my life, and that sense of purpose found its way into my movement helping me get through hours upon hours of flying, airports, security, customs and thousands of transitions. Yes I think with having typing available during all of the trips I could make my needs, feelings, and thoughts known to serious minded professors, not so serious minded film crew, likeable fellow typers dealing out witty statements, and connecting with people of different cultures. I think the accommodation of communication helped me the most to regulate and maintain calmness, showing the world my intelligence.

It has been the most wonderful time of my career as a self-advocate. Larry and I were awarded the Theresa Wood Citizenship Award at the Green Mountain Self-Advocates Voices and Choices Conference in May 2011. Then in 2013 I was mighty shocked to be awarded the Master Trainer award from the Institute on Communication and Inclusion at Syracuse University. Inclusion in meeting with top notch trainers who value my experience has been one key to my success.

With supported typing my life has transformed to one of purpose and independence; I have had opportunities to travel the globe spreading the message of inclusion and advocating for the right to communicate. My communication is paramount to my well-being and is key to my being an active citizen. I may appear to be a man shrouded by a cloak of incompetence but if you will take the time to listen to my typing you will understand I am intelligent. Yes, we need to speak up loud and clear, my typing friends. We are on the typing freedom train, moving our message around the country, teaching people that we have an intelligent voice.

Reflection Questions:
1. Tracy had the enthusiasm to learn self-advocacy skills but "needed direction from others who were doing this type of work." Who can you turn to for mentoring in self-advocacy? What are the self-advocacy skills you hope to strengthen?
2. Tracy was given the opportunity to travel abroad to Sri Lanka, Japan, and Finland. Which countries have you been or desire to go to? What is it about those countries that are special?

21 LISA VALLADO

Lisa Vallado
Maryland
23 years old

Highlights:
- Starred in the award-winning documentary, "Sisterly"
- Graduated with an associate degree
- Travelled abroad to Iceland by herself with her sisters

I am a 23-year old woman with autism who went to college to pursue a degree in Biology, and work in the field of neuroscience research. I am fighting every day to have the same opportunities as my peers in higher education and employment. I was the first student at Montgomery College, Maryland, to use a letter board and a communication partner.

I was born in Brazil and moved to the U.S. with my family when I was five years old. My journey started by first attending special education classes, having many IEPs, and being told not to have too many expectations about my future. My parents decided to take a different route by pulling me out of public school and enrolling me in a private Christian school that was willing to take a chance in learning how to create an inclusive environment on their campus. I was in second grade and stayed on their program until high school. Even though I was fully included in their program, my curriculum was modified. I was not working on the same academic level as my peers. I had limited communication skills, struggled with fine-motor skills, and sensory overload. My journey to college was not an easy one since I did not start communicating on a letter board until I was a sophomore in high school. This was a turning point in my life because it changed my path from a certificate of completion to a high school diploma. It was not an easy road, but it was a successful one because it created a path for many other students with autism after me. Words come out of my mouth by impulses and compulsions, but very seldom do they express what I am thinking. Learning to spell on a letter board allowed me to conquer the basic human right to have a voice and to be heard. My outlook on life changed from despair to life with endless possibilities, because at that moment, I found my voice.

I started college by taking only one class, and my first day was a collection of feelings of accomplishments and dreams coming true. I added a course each semester until I started taking three classes. In spring 2019, I graduated with my associate degree in Life Science, and I am applying to transfer to University of Maryland for a Biology degree. My favorite classes are science labs, and they are also the most challenging ones for my body. Sometimes I do get frustrated, and tears flow down my face without any control. However, with each class that I finish, I get more control over my body and more confidence about achieving my goals. My professors have been incredibly supportive and creative about finding new ways that I can be included and successful. Every time I have an interaction with my professors or classmates, I hope to plant a seed of inclusion, acceptance, new possibilities, and equality for all. Last year I was inducted into Phi Theta Kappa Honor Society, Kappa Omega Chapter, and I was nominated by my professor to apply for a NIST (National Institute of Standards and Technology) internship. When I started college, I would stay only an hour or so on campus. Now my longer days are 12 hours, and those are the happiest ones.

Getting an education is very important to me, however, having meaningful relationships in my life is very important as well. It is hard making friends when you are different, but I can say that the few friends that I have are the best in the world. I am blessed with a wonderful family that loves me and supports my dreams. On February 2017, I traveled to Iceland with my sisters. It was the most extraordinary trip of my life because I felt a glimpse of independence. It was the first time I went on a trip without my parents. My dream of doing amazing adventures with my sisters came true. I long for the freedom to do things like any other young adult - traveling, going out with friends, driving, going to college, having a job, and living on my own.

I am actively involved in advocating for access to higher education for women with disabilities and individuals with autism. According to the UNESCO data, "women with disabilities are often less likely to reap the benefits of a formal education than disabled men – marginalized not only by their disability but also by their gender." Last year I presented in two local conferences in Maryland, sharing my journey to college and encouraging others to never give up on their dreams. I was a special guest speaker at Delta Phi Epsilon Sorority at American University in Washington D.C. I am a board member at Reach Every Voice, a non-profit organization in Maryland supporting individuals who spell or type to communicate. This spring I am participating as a guest with a group of friends in a public health class with emphasis on autism at George Washington University. I was also the subject in the short documentary film,

"Sisterly," a finalist for the Student Academy Awards in 2017, and the winner of more than twenty awards in the U.S. and abroad.

My goal is to live a life filled with meaning and purpose. In one of my papers for my art class, I wrote about Michelangelo's sculpture David. I liked the fact that it is a naked sculpture, not because of the sexual appeal, but what it represents to me. King David was a powerful, rich, strong Bible character that defeated Goliath. Nevertheless, he was still just a man, a human being just like me. A naked figure also represents an authentic version of yourself. You are not hiding behind your clothes, status, degrees, fame, or power. It is the essence of who you are. I identify with this piece because I feel that people cover my body with all their assumptions and can no longer see the naked, authentic version of me. They can only see the image they created with all the layers they have added. They see their version of me, not who I am. I am working hard every day to create an authentic version of myself. I have goals to continue my education, pursue a career in neuroscience, and live independently. If you are going to dream, shoot for the stars. Because as you get higher each day, your view gets better, your problems look smaller, and the journey makes you stronger.

Reflection Questions:
1. Lisa had the opportunity to travel with her sisters on her own to Iceland. If you could invite any friends or family members to go with you on a trip abroad, who would you take and where would you go?
2. Lisa emphasizes the importance of creating "an authentic version of myself" and describes the goals she plans to pursue to achieve authenticity. What would an authentic version of yourself mean? What goals would help you achieve your own version of authenticity?

INNOVATORS, FOUNDERS, AND CREATORS

22 EMMA CLADIS

Emma Cladis
California
21 years old

Highlights:

- Co-founded the Friendship Circle in southern California
- University student
- National conference speaker

I think I will highlight what comes to mind about my very short but amazing life so far. I learned to type at six years old thanks to Soma Mukhopadhyay, my first typing teacher. That is when my life changed from slipping into autism's silence to engaging with the world. I worked hard to prove it was me communicating by more and more independent typing. I was mainstreamed into second grade and have stayed in typical classes ever since. During elementary school it was a time of learning and sharing the good hope of what was possible for a non speaking autistic typer.

Somewhere around 2005 I met a wonderful person, my next typing mentor, Darlene Hanson. She and I still work together today. Mostly now it is on my speech since I am becoming more and more verbal. She has been my guide from apraxia to speech; chaos to communicating, by typing and now verbalizing.

In 2009, I was awarded the Yes I Can! Award, for academic excellence from the Council of Exceptional Children. They flew me to Seattle and I got to share my story. This great conference experience began my passion for advocating for all people who have differences. I love bringing hope where there is sadness.

Since then over the years, I have had many amazing opportunities to present at schools and conferences; including Pepperdine University, Chapman University, Cal State Long Beach, in their psychology clubs and classes, Profectum Conferences, College Bound Academy and most recently, at California TASH, and my own University, Vanguard.

These presentations each have given me a sense of respect that I have something important to share with others and a different way of giving what I know to be true to many people. I believe the listeners in-turn have been changed and then go on to challenge others in their thinking and positions on special needs.

I have a webpage called www.hopeneverending.com where you can find my story and the works of books and videos I have authored. I am blessed to have a dad who is an artist and we have collaborated on a couple of books. He has illustrated and put pictures to my words.

One of my most proud accomplishments is Friendship Group. When I was ten years old I was one of the founders of the group and it still thrives today. It is this wonderful safe place for typers to come and socialize. Something that we autistic non speakers are not suppose to be interested in doing. This has been a place to support each other and find understanding and courage.

In 2016, I graduated high school with a diploma and honors. And, against all odds because of health difficulties, began my college career the following fall. I'm now in my third year at Vanguard University and loving it there. I am Vanguard's first non speaking autistic student on campus, studying as a communications major to become a film screenwriter.

Being on a college campus is a dream come true; really, there is so much to tell you about this experience. The time there gives me the opportunity to interact with others in whole new ways, to open their minds to this different kind of person, and then begin to see me and the world a bit differently and with a lot more compassion. I want to give this campus my heart and show them what it is like to be really hopeful and see the world the way I do. Our differences together can create something new, something beautiful. We have so much to give.

My plans are to produce documentaries about our typing community in order to bring better understanding to us and the need for more inclusion and opportunities in education and careers. I also hope to write movies full of goodness and joy to bring to this sad world. I want to do a great work for God in my lifetime. I seldom miss an opportunity to advocate for my autistic typing community and my films will just open up more ways to do this. In these ways I will share hope with so many and bring to this world light that will open hearts and minds.

I really want to say, that all of this is only possible because God is with me.

Reflection Questions:
1. Emma was flown to Seattle to share her story at a conference. Imagine you were offered to speak at a conference. To which city would you fly? What would be your message to the conference audience?
2. Emma aspires to produce documentaries and films for her future career. If you were to create

documentaries or movies, what would they be about? What theme or storyline would you highlight in the film?

23 NICHOLAS D'AMORA

Nicholas D'Amora
New York
21 years old

Highlights:
- Founder of a social group for people who type and spell that turned into a habilitation day program
- Conference speaker and award winner
- Trained his teacher team on how to support his communication methods

Ten years ago, I met a woman named Soma Mukhopadhyay who would change my life forever. I am Nick, I am 21 and I have non-speaking autism. There were many times in my life I thought I would never have the opportunity to speak. Then I learned the rapid prompting method (RPM) method down in Texas—and that opportunity was never again doubted. Soma opened my world and gave me the key to unlock every challenging door I was facing. I learned to communicate, the most freeing obstacle in my life. Since that time, I've been practicing my spelling and teaching my body how to cooperate which has been a difficult struggle.

My spelling skills were improving and with that my communication grew. I now had a voice and a way to reach the world. When I was little, I knew I was different. My first recollection was when I joined a typical preschool. I could see that the other kids had more control over their bodies and everything seemed so easy for them. I knew at that point I was going to have to fight hard in order to keep up and fit in. Having autism is a minute-by-minute challenge and people don't realize that my body is a total disorganized mess. My impulsive movements, stims, and complete lack of control at times, can be exhausting. There are times though that I feel autism is a gift and I see it as my way in which to advocate for myself and others like me. Ever since I have learned to communicate I've been wanting to find many ways to tell my story and spread awareness about how autism works.

When I began this advocacy journey I was terrified and nervous. I was not only nervous about my own abilities to speak out, but terrified about what the public's opinions were about me. I remember thinking there is so much I've doubted about myself and how am I going to convince others that I am intelligent, have the ability to speak for myself, and am not disabled in my mind.

There were moments when I wanted to give up and stay hidden and run away from the truth. But I had so many people encouraging and supporting me, I knew it was time to start helping others at that point. I had to put my fears aside and start living for myself. If I wanted to grow more independent, I needed to face the world and tell my story. I've since done numerous speeches, conferences, and seminars. I've spoken to schools, committees, agencies colleges, and doctors. Surprisingly, they all listened and accepted what I was saying. For the first time large amounts of people were finally listening to me and I was amazed. This gave me the courage and determination to keep going.

I was no longer afraid but overwhelmed with joy that I was being accepted into this world!

I continued this work and still today I am asked to speak and educate. I am no longer fearful but sometimes I am frustrated by it. I enjoy telling my story but I become reluctant when all listen to me but no action is taken. I've reached a point in my life where I want to turn my story into something more productive. I've been acknowledged and have received honorary awards for my accomplishments. I think my greatest achievement however was the opening of a social group in my area where other spellers got together to support, learn, and grow along side one another. From this, a new adult day habilitation program began! It involves teaching adults with respect by forming their own opinions and living a life for themselves.

I've also been proud of my achievements at school. I fought eagerly to advise NYC BOE Administrators that this support was necessary to place it on my individualized education plan (IEP) goals. I requested that my teachers, therapists, paras, and all other staff learn about this method and that I needed this type of education and communication in my everyday life. In order for that to happen I had to train all of my teachers about this method and how to work with me. Self-advocacy paid off once again and now I felt able to start planning my life and what goals I wanted to accomplish. Doors were opening for me and I've learned job skills, cooking in restaurants, learning how to make meals, socializing with the community and taking on an algebra class in a typical high school. I've continued to take the high road, not giving up on my dreams. I've done so much in a short time. This year my ultimate dream has come true. My persistence and involvement with the autism community has given me the greatest reward. I am being honored by On Your Mark, an agency here on Staten Island for adult services. I've been asked to participate in a presentation for being one of its founders and am being honored at their yearly gala. You have to understand these type of awards have never been given to anyone with autism. They have always been reserved for politicians and corporate type people. So you could imagine the joy and triumph that I am feeling right now! I am determined to continue this path to find a better way to right our rights to promote awareness to change the mindset to give all people equal opportunities—to never give in and to never give up on yourself and live.

Reflection Questions:

1. Nick reflects on gaining independence in his narrative. He says, "If I wanted to grow more independent, I needed to face the world and tell my story." What do you need to face to become more independent in your own life? Fill in blank from your own perspective: "If I want to grow more independent, I need to _____."

2. To ensure that Nick's team of teachers supported his everyday communication, he "had to train all of my teachers about this method and how to work with me." If you were in charge of training your teachers or support providers, what would you include in your training manual? What are the key points you would cover in your training?

24 JUSTICE KILLEBREW

Justice Killebrew
California
13 years old

Highlights:
- Created a t-shirt line called "What's J Say?"
- Award winning poet at the state level
- Featured in a Los Angeles Times story

The odds were stacked against me at a very early age. I was diagnosed with autism at age 2 1/2. My pediatrician told my parents there was nothing wrong with me. However, my parents thought differently. That's when I met Amanda, my first Behavior Intervention Associate, who was a pivotal part of my new journey. She was supportive, challenging, and also assertive. She believed in me!

Ms. Denise, my speech language pathologist, was the first to diligently work towards effective communication. When I became preschool age I attended DuValle Educational Center. Four beautiful women were dedicated to setting high standards for me and treating me like everyone else. Ms. Debbie, Ellery, Meeks, and Kara challenged me daily with life skills and work routines.

At the age of 5, I moved to California. A new journey awaited as I embarked upon my new life. The beginning was a bit challenging as I had to get adjusted to a new home, school, and environment. Nevertheless, I gave it my best shot. My kindergarten class was not much of a challenge because I was accustomed to more independence than what they allowed. I wasn't typing at that time and my communication was limited to my teacher talking at me as if I couldn't comprehend. The frustration I felt lasted four grueling years! In those four years we tried sign language, and PECS, but we weren't successful.

It wasn't until 2015 that my life changed forever! My mom was watching a documentary entitled, "A Mother's Courage: Talking Back to Autism," on Netflix one afternoon. She explained the movie so vividly to my Pops as I listened. It was about a mother who unlocked her child's voice. My mom was so inspired that she spoke to my applied behavioral analysis (ABA) team, Karla and Kristen, about it. The supervisor of the agency had expressed she knew a mom who had taken this same journey and was successful! My Mom contacted Tami Barmache, Dillan Barmache's mom, and my journey began to take flight.

We waited 6 months to finally meet my "Voice Angel," Soma Mukhopadhyay, who unlocked my voice in one 25 minute session! My first words to my family were, "I'm glad you cracked my case." I was excited to share my thoughts, feelings, likes and dislikes with my family after all of these years!

Katie and Lindsey picked up where Soma left off since she lives in Texas and I live in California. They talked to me and not at me, and engaged me in meaningful conversations. They would ask my political views and flood my mind with facts and data! They genuinely asked my thoughts and opinions, and respected my goals, ambitions, and high hopes!

Elementary school was the most challenging phase of my education, because no one knew or cared to learn how to properly communicate with me. It wasn't until 6th grade that I finally had a teacher who trusted my communication-by-typing process! I was a very fluent typer at home and in the community but at school my voice was silent. Ms. Duncan saw more in me than my behaviors and decided to challenge me. She helped develop my literary skills which allowed me to enter my poem into the National Parent Teacher Association Reflections contest, and make it to the state level! I was the 1st African American special needs artist in the history of Glendale Unified School District to ever make it to state! My Principal, Dr. Bruich announced it over the intercom. I was so ecstatic because I was also interviewed by the LA Times!

Even though things are more positive because of my ability to communicate I still at times have anxious thoughts. That's where my therapist, Nate, comes in. He supports me with exercises to tame my anxious thoughts.

I love math, science, language arts, and I love to create. In addition to being a poet, I am also a D.J., I play basketball, and I have a t-shirt line called "What's J Say?" I created this to advocate for and empower people like myself.

I can truly say that I am breaking the societal barriers that are placed upon me. I will continue to represent my people well and advocate for the voiceless! I hope to inspire fellow typers by sharing my journey. I hope to set an example to stay optimistic! Believe in yourself! I am a History-Maker with Autism.

Let's change the world together, one heart at a time!

Reflection Questions:
1. Justice created a t-shirt line called "What's J Say?" If you were to create your own t-shirt line, what would you call it?
2. Justice is the first African American student with a

disability who made it to the state level of his school's writing contest. Why do the intersections of these two identities (African American and disability) make his accomplishment even more significant?

25 LUKAS MCALLISTER

Lukas McAllister
California
23 years old

Highlights:
- Founded "Luke's Packet Ministry" through his church
- His project was featured in publications and earned him the 2019 Grand Marshall role for the Autism Society of Ventura County

I have carried autism with me my whole life. My story has many tsunami-type challenges. Muddy waters of autism emerge even when my brain is a clear blue ocean. Becoming a necessary member of society has been my grounding guide for making the world more valuable. The beginning idea that I am necessary formed when I learned to express my thoughts through slow, methodical spelling. When I learned to spell I had great challenges. It was really important to not give up.

Since I was small, I have intensely resented autism. Calamity struck and I found myself healing after a lung biopsy, yet losing agility. This was when I began fighting my body. Then came my autism diagnosis.

A shadowy cast of despair was darkening my hopeful heart. Trying to teach myself to control my autism has been a barrier I continually overcome. Merely steering in my desired direction jars my stubborn autistic impulses. I need constant supplications to support spelling.

Working with Soma, and her constant prompting, helped me control my body enough that I could start to prove that I was smart. Since I liked animals I responded to learning about them really well when I was younger. I communicated my responses through using choices, hard as it was learning in this way. Teachers were not trained to support my communication. I was given easy lessons that were boring. I started homeschooling so that my lessons could be at grade level.

Given a communication lesson I needed calm instruction including clear feedback about strategies that let me control my body to type. Calming strategies allowed communication to improve. I needed someone I could trust to stay calm too. Since I got tired easily while spelling, I needed constant reminders to regulate myself.

Even now, tasks give me immense difficulty because I have motor challenges. Getting exercise is crucial to regulation. I also need calm, helpful moments of reading in between moments of spelling. Calming strategies are necessary because anxiety paralyzes my dreams.

Yet some dreams are coming true.

One dream I had was to attend college.

I almost managed to find my direction but obstacles kept interrupting including severe sinus pain. I really needed consistent communication. Inability to communicate considerably hampered my basic goals to generate my thoughts on academic topics. Judgment of my faculty for critical thinking kept getting in the way. I doubted myself. This doubt clung onto me tirelessly. Yet I valued my wit and knowledge. My light inside pushed through darkness. Judgment started to fade. Riding light's galloping momentum allowed myself to eventually tackle college.

I needed to get my limitations explained, leading me to inquire about support services at my local college. Access to necessary accommodations required meeting with a specialist in the disability office. I had serious resistance in class. Lectures gave me difficulty, challenging my ability to sit still. I needed breaks. Caring about noises in the classroom instead of learning, my instructor made me embarrassed. Challenging behaviors connected to my autism is not inclusion. My concerns get amplified like a stacked up house of cards ready to collapse.

I needed a calm environment so I could reach my full potential. Cheery environments help generate hope for sufficient growth, like the rain brings beautiful green hills after horrible fires. Needing instruction on more interesting topics led me to try online classes. Constant severe jaw pain almost derailed my ability to do classes, but I finally got a doctor to listen and recommend oral surgery to relieve the pain. While the transition for someone who types to communicate was not easy, I have been successfully completing college classes.

Another dream I had was to advocate for others.

Since I care greatly for needy individuals, I started a "packet ministry" four years ago that provides bags of food, supplies, and scriptures that give a message of hope. I would see the needy with their signs on street corners, and I wanted to help. Being autistic, I especially sensed how to empathize with desolation. The real genius of this ministry is that I was able to organize it with members at the Camarillo Church of Christ so that the congregation would never run out of these "packets." Funded by donations and the benevolence committee, supplies are ordered in bulk and constantly replenished so that members are able to give out packets and always have more available. My leadership has been gaining momentum, motivating my community and beyond, to create hundreds of packets that are given out annually.

This project was featured in The Christian Chronicle and also in Outreach Magazine, as well as being on exhibit at Pepperdine University's Harbor Bible Lectures. It was also featured at the Ventura County Autism Society's Aut2Run, where I was honored to be chosen as the 2019 Grand Marshall.

Inspired by the Good Samaritan story in the book of Luke, we now have an official logo for this project, calling it "Luke's Packet Ministry," with the theme verse from Luke 10:37. Details about this ministry can be found on the church website at camarillochurchofchrist.com. In the future I would like to start a nonprofit company to help the needy.

My other area of advocacy is for those with autism. Since I also want to impact autism studies, I'm employed part-time by NYU to contribute to autism research. Some of these studies are being conducted in my own community.

In order to meet the challenges in my life, I need reminders that allow me to claim important messages giving me inspiration. I like listening to scriptures that give hope and biographies that show real people overcoming difficult circumstances. I want to thank all those on my team who have helped me implement successful strategies; I rely on my team. This team of communication partners, therapists, family, and friends helped me to make an impact.

Now I feel more confident than ever that I can do this. Remember challenges can make you stronger.

Reflection Questions:
1. Lukas faced many challenges in the college classroom, from contending with his own uncooperative body to dealing with unsupportive instructors. What advice would you give to Lukas'

instructors to help them be more supportive to a student like Lukas?

2. Lukas started a "packet ministry" at his church to help individuals in need. He saw a need in the community that he felt he could meet. Identify a need in the community and describe the steps you would take to meet the need.

26 E.J. O'CONNOR

E.J. O'Connor
California
12 years old

Highlights:
- Serves in the unique role of autistic peer-advocate on individualized education plans (IEPs) for other students
- A multi-modal communicator who uses symbol-based apps, keyboards, and letter boards
- Gained access to these communication tools at the early age of 9 with multiple communication partners

When I was 8 I showed I could read by matching pictures to words. My mom had seen a video about alternative teaching and gave it a try. I couldn't draw lines on worksheets to match words and pictures at that time but I could work with cut-out pictures and words. Not completely sure why, but I think multiple senses working together helped me. I always loved letters and would trace them on signs when I saw them. Soon after, I started typing words that I liked after someone showed me how to slow down a bit by holding back my hand. When she let go I just kept typing. My favorite words from videos just stream out. The typing is what "earned" me an AAC evaluation. I was given a system called LAMP but the school couldn't handle it, so I started using TouchChat. It's great for basic wants and needs and I still use it til now. I can use this system with anyone so that comes in handy. Then mommy read *Ido in Autismland* and decided to pursue RPM.

We did nightly lessons right into the iPad for about 3 months and hit a wall when approaching more age appropriate stuff. Early on I refused to go back to school because I was bored and scared (mostly of being treated like I wasn't smart). We flew to Soma in January 2016 when I was 9 and the stencils helped me slow down and get each letter out. Her confidence, support and energy made me confident. It was truly the beginning of a life with more possibilities. For the next 6 months mommy and I did nightly lessons on the stencil. It was much harder but I enjoyed learning real stuff. In June of 2016, we went back to Soma and I was able to show math and writing like poems and stories.

It took Mommy and family about 10 months to catch up and be able to support me but along the way we did interesting lessons and spent so much quality time together. Even when I would walk away Mommy told everyone to keep reading to me. I was listening but needed to keep myself moving. It actually helps me to listen. It is much harder to listen if I can't move.

Soon after Mommy became good at supporting me, Meredith, my amazing stepmom, joined us at another Soma camp and then she was able to support me. I wrote this next part with her. Her dedication and love have helped me so much.

I spell with several communication partners. It makes me start to generalize my skill. My greatest thing is to be able to communicate with my friends for growth in my skill. It is my motivation.

I try communicating now with as many partners as I possibly can so I will always be able to communicate. It first is hard to start spelling with a new person because we don't know how to work together yet.

I can also communicate on the boards with my whole family. They have different energies so it's not always easy but I feel their love and that helps.

This next part was written with my friend, Julie, who is now my school assigned AT (Assistive Technology) person. She has that gentle confidence that makes my words flow. She asked my thoughts on being a leader. I am lucky to be among this group of leaders who have shaped my journey in such a beautiful way.

Being a leader plays an important role in our community. Our historical leaders have been people who thought they understood autism from an outside perspective. Today's leaders have an inside perspective. I will make sure to let people know how their expectations make people step up or step down. I have experienced both high and low expectations. You can see a huge change in my abilities from when people had low expectations and from when those expectations became higher. My abilities have always been here. People with low expectations only see disability. My abilities were born through high expectations.

My mom and I have attended and helped in many IEPs now. We have been able to get low tech AAC and letterboards on IEPs so friends can be exposed to real material and allowed to spell in school. I am grateful to be homeschooled especially after hearing about the uphill battles many of my friends are facing. Some families are not able to homeschool so we try to provide a better option then repetitive drills and preschool material.

I hope my story is helpful and hopeful.

Reflection Questions:

1. E.J. is able to communicate with multiple communication partners, whereas most individuals who communicate on a keyboard or letter board only have access to one communication partner. What do you feel would be the advantages and challenges to having multiple communication partners?

2. E.J. says, "My abilities were born through high expectations." Describe a time in which high expectations were set for you and you rose to the occasion.

27 JOHN-CARLOS SCHAUT

John-Carlos Schaut
Wisconsin
22 years old

Highlights:

- Co-created "Sanctuary," an interdenominational church to support individuals who use letterboards and keyboards
- Transitioned from a self-contained education to Honors English
- Attends college

I was born at home with a natural start. I walked and talked early and then at 3 ½ years I slipped inside until I came out again. I visited and worked with Soma Mukhopadhyay, finding my voice with rapid prompting method (RPM). I learned to find each letter on the board, all along having so much to say. I started school in a self-contained school and stayed there until Mrs. Owens gave me a big break in 7th-grade science when I spelled "ultraviolet." I graduated from high school with a 3.8 GPA in 2016 after taking Honors English, Chemistry, and Algebra.

They all said it could not be done, but it was done! Amen! Angels flooded my caretakers and communication partners to assist me to graduate with distinguished high honors in community service and a wonderful academic belief in my authorship.

I have a friend, Aaron. He stands with me. In high school, he came with me to an IEP to advocate for me about sensory and movement issues. For five years, together we lead and were inspired to create "Sanctuary," an interdenominational church for our people. We spell out our talks to encourage our folks who are suffering in body/sensory or intense despair. We celebrate victories.

Summer camp: Camp Hermon was our inspiration. We have 6 trained RPM partners and campers that gather for socials in a refreshing outdoor setting. We spend time together in a real community of love and respect. I help lead homilies for support and hope. The volunteers are changed forever. We are a force for good in the world; change agents like no other!

College has brought many challenges. In high school, because of my high GPA and great advocacy, I was recommended by school administrators to attend the Youth Options early college program. I was admitted to Carthage College here in Kenosha, WI. I liked the idea of studying anthropology. I believed that I could add a unique perspective of disability on all peoples, in the science of human beings. I believed the class would benefit with a typer/speller in their midst. We would learn so much from each other. I had a longtime communication partner, Carol Manthei, all ready to assist. I went to orientation, had my books and my ID. At the last minute, I was pulled from the class by the" Director of Learning Accessibility.". Although the director refused to meet me, she questioned the validity of my authorship. She would let me attend but receive no credit; I could only audit the class. No thank you! We filed a civil rights suit and I found another college: Regent University Early College Program. They were happy to have me. Since then, I tried other options to attend college on campus, but I am now enrolled in the University of The People.

I have learned to never give up. I am an outlier; an overcomer. I have goals to open an art business with the help of my family, and my communication partner, Heather Robinson. We go to a program called "Garden Works" where we design, plant, harvest and create soaps and products from the harvest. I have learned about natural dyes and plan to use this for a fiber arts business. Heather is a person who believes in me. She calms me and will hunt me down to do my best. Heather is sweet and tough as nails. How can I ever say "thank you" enough?!

I have overcome oppression and oppressive people. I have a great family as my support team. When I was young and my autism struck I lost the ability to say words, but I never lost "Sophia." Sophia is a big blessing and she "gets me." Sophie is my bossy older sister I am most blessed to have. She is hard to say "no" to and she gets the job done. Sophia is a nurse and is winning Daisey awards for excellence in nursing all because of me! She always says she trained at the feet of the master (me). She has done so much for me and has led me into the world. I could never be where I am if not for you.

Isaac is my brother who makes me laugh. He says he has a "little bit of autism." Sometimes I wish we could converse easily as other brothers do; still, he is my car partner going for rides around town to get iced teas. These are simple nightly pleasures that bring meaning to our lives. Thank you for being my brother!

Shu Lan, my younger sister, is the only family member with a higher GPA than me. Shu helps out and is so gifted at our Camp Hermon, for our community. Thank you for your love and help.

In ending I will close with a quote by Margaret Meade:

"Never doubt that a few thoughtful committed citizens could change the world. Indeed, it's the only thing that ever did."

Reflection Questions:

1. John-Carlos co-created an interdenominational church that was inclusive of people who type and spell to communicate. What changes or innovations would you create in religious settings (yours or others) to improve inclusion and belonging for autistic individuals?
2. John-Carlos' siblings play an important role in his life. What do you enjoy about your relationships with your siblings or cousins?

UNIVERSITY AND
COLLEGE STUDENTS

28 NICOLAS JONCOUR

Nicolas Joncour
France
19 years old

Highlights:
- Only publicly known college student who types to communicate in the country of France
- Participant in the European Movement for Independent Living

I was born 19 years ago in France where segregation and institutions are the reality for disabled people and especially for nonverbal autistic people like me.

My life was peaceful for the first 9 years. I only had a few hours of school during the week, and even though I received speech therapy and an aide at school, I didn't feel different from the other students. The fact I was autistic and nonverbal didn't affect me very much. My parents loved me and all my family treated me very well. I knew I was different but I didn't suffer from it. It was later that I understood that my parents had been fighting for me to stay in school, as no one apart from the speech therapist was aware of my capabilities. In 3rd grade, my parents hired a tutor who came to my home to help me with academics and who understood my capabilities. My teacher at school believed her and it was a very good year with a great and wonderful aide. But, there was conflict in the school between teachers, especially after my teacher left my school for another position. When I was in 4th grade the headmaster of my school made me leave the school. I realised I couldn't count on people to support me; I had to succeed by myself.

My parents have always supported me unconditionally. I began to understand their investment in me only recently by observing how other nonverbal acquaintances were treated by their parents. The reality of these autists in France is terrible and they become soulless beings, abandoned in psychiatric hospitals. I've seen and heard terrible testimonies about their conditions. They have never had access to education and their situation makes you so dizzy it is beyond imaginable.

I had been homescholing for three years before I asked to come back to middle school. I like to be with others and I could not stand being separated from children my age. The middle school near home was very welcoming. I had a hard time typing with my aides, and it was pretty frustrating. In France, non-speaking autistic students are not mainstreamed and the aides and the teachers at school are not trained to support any disabilities and AAC (even in picture exchange communication system, PECS) and it is not possible to choose the aide.

I would call myself a very sociable person, but being unable to communicate with others made me want to stay with my parents. I was taking home school courses at the same time with the CNED (correspondence courses of the Ministry of National Education, with certified teachers). I was having trouble typing with other people than my mother (even though I was typing with my speech therapist and psychologist) and my dependence on my mom came at a cost. I always had to express myself in my mom's presence.

At age 11, I talked about my faith to my parents who are atheists. I had been very interested in the Holocaust since I was 10 years old, and this has led me to Christ. Christ helped me to lead my life through obstacles. I was baptized at 15 years old. Faith is my hammer against the obstacles of life. This hammer, this faith, opposes the weakness found in souls who live without love.

I sought out other opportunities for growth. When I was 15 I took piano lessons with Henny Kupferstein who became like my mentor. These classes were taken online. She is marvelous. Few people believe in me like she does.

I began to go to a home high school for a few hours with an aide who was not trained to communicate with me. The high school definitely made me understand how much I loved being with others. I really wanted to attend high school in person full time, but not all of my helpers could communicate with me. And I had to continue the home school courses that I loved too.

I was 16 years old when I understood that the Departmental Home for people with disabilities had decided not to give me an aide I need at school, which is indispensable to help me to regulate. Instruction is obligatory until 16 years old and the Departmental Home for people with disabilities was reluctant to let me continue in the mainstream system. I felt so bad that I was motivated to write an article about my experience and the delay of France about autism. The article was published in the online newspaper, ZOOM.

Despite my challenges in high school, I persisted in achieving my educational goals. In 2017, I became the first French nonspeaking autistic student to pass the exam, the "Baccalauréat," which is needed to go to university in France. I enrolled in college to pursue a physics degree.

Everything changed at college as you can employ your own personal assistant. My life began to be the one I dreamed of. I spent the day in college with my communication partners whom we had chosen and trained. We were not given the opportunity to choose and train our own aides before this. I finally had friends, and I developed more and more autonomy. This feeling of independence had a taste of justice and revenge against those who did not believe in me in the past. The faculty and students were nice and supportive. Although I learned over time that physics was not for me, I reoriented myself to earn a degree in law.

Since 2016, I belong to the European Movement for Independent Living (EMIL) Youth Network. In 2018, I went to an EMIL study session in Strausberg during a week with my aide. It was entitled, "Active Citizenship and Political Participation of Young Disabled People as a Pathway Towards Independent Living." It was wonderful to meet other young disabled people from all over Europe, and talk about self determination, empowerment, with the slogan "nothing about us without us."

I love law studies. Even if I have to keep on fighting for my rights, I live the life I choose and I want to help other non-speaking autistic people to gain their independence.

Reflection Questions:
1. Nico is a trailblazer in the country of France for being one of the only students who types to communicate. If you could travel to any country to show others what it's like to type or spell to communicate, what country would you visit and why?
2. Nico had trouble finding the right communication partner to support him in school at various times in his life. What are the qualities you look for in a communication partner to support strong communication?

29 KAEGAN SMITH
MAN ON FIRE

Kaegan Smith
Colorado
22 years old

Highlights:

- Online college student
- Began communicating with a letter board at 18
- Aims to be a leader in sustainability

A guy meets a pretty girl and, suddenly, his body falls to the floor as he yells, "BURNING MAN!" You mean, that's not how it went for you? Maybe not literally, but I bet figuratively, you can relate. For me, it was both figurative and literal. I felt like my heart and lungs were on fire when I met her, so guess what my body's reaction was? Yep, Burning Man threw himself to the floor, yelling and sizzling.

(Parents: How many times have you watched your autistic child "tantrum" and thought of their actions as disconnected or random?)

My eight-year-old body stood screaming and unable to

move at the fun end-of-year, school carnival. I refused to cooperate. This was exactly what I had feared and as my mother drug me home, I screamed louder. I wanted desperately to participate, but, as often happened, my body reacted opposite of what I wanted.

(Educators: How many times has your autistic student reacted in a confusing way?)

I was traveling and having a wonderful trip when suddenly, I heard it. The loudest, most sudden intrusion invaded my consciousness. The unspeakable, that which shall not be named. The wildest and unfathomable chaos filled my senses.

A baby cried somewhere far in the back of the plane. I thought I would be able to hold myself together until I heard myself screaming.

I was mortified to be an adult man, screaming, and I was trapped 30,000 feet in the sky. You may imagine yourself screaming uncontrollably with no escape and for seemingly no reason. This can be my reality in the blink of an eye -- or in this case, in the cry of a baby.

I am over-empathetic. I simply cannot take the hysterics of others without creating hysterics of my own. In those moments, I feel completely unlovable. I am aware of my disturbance and of how I must appear. It terrifies me, and you know how helpful fear can be...so the problem is perpetuated.

(Fellow Autistics: Can you relate?)

These are a few examples of how my body betrays my mind. Almost without fail, I am failed by my body. My life was spent knowing that my body would act in opposition to my brain. Is it any wonder those like me are frustrated and seem to act out?

This is not the end of my story, though.

I was eighteen years old when my life changed. The Rapid Prompting Method, developed by Soma Mukhopadhyay, was a lifeline I could, and still, cling to. Learning to communicate by spelling using a simple letter board would save me from silence. I was awarded the gift of hope wrapped in academic lessons that matched my intellectual ability. The way I learned to express my thoughts has become my way out of solitude.

Communication is everything. I am now an accomplished traveler, able to convince my over-reactive body to calm down by spelling self commands. When my body reacts to fear in ways that betray me, I use my communication method to conquer those fears. I am able to express my feelings and desires and, in so doing, lean into life. I can communicate my fears, following the train of thought all the way to the end and realize the solution. I am able to ask for aid and advice. Voicing visualization by spelling what I want to manifest in my life has led to victories over many fears.

In addition to conquering fears and gaining the voice to explain my wayward body, I am also enabled to direct my own life. I am an online college student, studying Sustainability Science. With this line of study, my intention is to use my interest in preservation to aid in community development for others like myself, with the desire to live sustainably. I hope to lead the autistic population toward communities where we can affect each other positively, and simultaneously, lesson the environmental footprint of humanity. This focus on mentorship and leadership is only possible because of communication. I am still a man on fire, only now, with purpose.

Reflection Questions:
1. Kaegan describes his alter ego as the Burning Man when his body doesn't cooperate with him. What would you name your alter ego when your body doesn't cooperate with you and why?
2. Kaegan uses his communication to conquer his fears over a body that betrays him. What strategies do you use to cope with emotional or physical reactions that betray you?

30 KAYLA TAKEUCHI
BORN IN SILENCE

Kayla Takeuchi
California
27 years old

Highlights:
- Earned an Associate of Arts degree
- Raised awareness about supporting students who type and spell to communicate at the community college level

I am a nonspeaking autistic who types to communicate. However, it wasn't always that way. I lived in silence for fifteen years until I met my angel, Janna Woods. Janna supported nonspeaking individuals like me to type. I first sat down with her on April 3, 2007 and that was the day I stepped out of silence and found my voice. I typed for three hours that day as my parents, being proper Japanese, sat in silence. That is, until we got in the car for the three-hour ride home and they expressed their astonishment. From that day forward, my life was forever changed.

Prior to finding my voice, I lived a life of frustration and despair. My parents took me to doctors and specialists who poked me with needles and ran countless tests to see why I was not speaking and throwing tantrums for no apparent reason. I love my parents so much for trying, but nothing that was suggested worked for me.

What I really wanted more than anything was a real education with textbooks and to be fully included with my peers. Instead, I was given PECS (Picture Exchange Communication System), which left me with no real way to have a conversation. After typing with Janna and feeling the freedom of having my own voice, I wanted to burn that book of PECS. My mother told the school personnel that it was not enough for me, but I was not allowed to type. I was able to take charge of my IEP meeting for two hours and nothing changed. The teachers and special education administrators did not believe in me, so I was relegated to being moved around like a piece of furniture and watching videos in class.

My parents and I decided to attend a different school district. We fought for my right to have a voice. We hired an attorney and went through due process, but unfortunately, we did not prevail.

The next chapter was waiting to be written. I went on home study for three months and I enrolled in a charter school where the administrators and teachers believed in me. There, my intellect was valued and respected. I graduated with a real diploma and I was able to help two nonspeaking friends enroll at the charter school.

I then enrolled in a community college after an encouraging meeting with a college recruiter. He believed in me from the beginning and assured me that my typing would not be questioned.

But more battles were ahead of me as I persevered to fight against barriers preventing many disabled college students from graduating. I enjoyed my classes and instructors at Clovis Community College (CCC), but I had much difficulty fulfilling the math requirement. The algebra class required that I "show my work," and I had no application on my iPad for this. I met with my counselor on a regular basis and I asked if another class could be substituted for the algebra class. CCC was a relatively new campus at the time and had no such policy for a unique student like me. Add to this the fact that I had three counselors in three years and received inconsistent information from each of them, and you can probably understand my frustration. Finally, it was recommended that I transfer to Fresno City College (FCC), where there is a large disabled student population. I was told the Disabled Students Programs and Services (DSP&S) department would be better able to help me with accommodations and support.

My new counselor, Leslie, immediately understood my mode of communication and set to work to help me fulfill my math requirement. This proved to be a very difficult task. Leslie talked with the math department dean, and she was only willing to offer alternate classes with a math prerequisite, even though I had the diagnosis of a learning disability in math. In good faith, I took a learning disabled math class, which turned out to be a disaster with the instructor teaching statistics, calculus, and pre-trigonometry instead of basic math concepts. Needless to say, I failed the class and my self-confidence fell to a new low. Leslie didn't give up on me and she kept advocating for me, enlisting the DSP&S director for more help.

I continued to take classes I enjoyed in the social sciences department while Leslie kept up her fight with the math department. Then, in January 2018, I met my FCC angel, my constitutional law instructor. I went to see Mr. Hill outside of class to ask about ideas for a research paper. As we talked, he asked me if I was a new student and what my educational goals were. My mom told Mr. Hill the shortened version of my FCC story and he immediately offered to help me with the math challenge. Mr. Hill is a former prosecutor and judge and current president of the faculty senate at FCC, so I began to feel some optimism that I might be able to graduate after all. After four months of intense advocating on my behalf, Mr. Hill was able to help me meet my graduation requirements. I am forever grateful to Mr. Hill and hope to continue our relationship in the years to come.

After four years of establishing relationships and self-advocacy, I received an Associates in Arts degree. Because discrimination was revealed, the college now has a committee with procedures in place to help students like me. I have a sense of accomplishment in knowing that other students will be able to graduate without the struggles I had.

My message to everyone is to presume competence in your nonspeaking friends. They are relying on your support to make their dreams come true. My fellow typers and spellers, please have the strength to persevere even during the darkest of times. Find the angels to support you and your lives will be transformed in ways you never thought possible.

Reflection Questions:
1. Kayla explains having to change from one school to another and from one community college to another to find the right educational environment. These transitions were both difficult yet helpful to Kayla. Describe a major change in your life that was both difficult and helpful to your success.
2. Kayla explains that her community "college now has a committee with procedures in place to help students like me" after realizing that Kayla experienced discrimination. What educational policies or practices have created barriers to your educational success? What do you propose educational leaders should do to solve the issue?

31 DAVID TEPLITZ

David Teplitz
California
23 years old

Highlights:
- First nonspeaking autistic to be admitted to University of California, Berkeley
- His advocacy has helped raise over $250,000 for autism research and awareness

When I learned to type at age five, my entire life changed for the better as I finally had a way to express my thoughts and feelings. It was really the breakthrough that I so desperately desired. My wonderful ABA therapist, Sabrina, and my speech therapist, Christy, devised a way for me to learn how to type to communicate. I never realized that this was unusual and that other nonspeaking autistics were not given this opportunity until much later. I was included in our local elementary school starting in kindergarten until 8th grade. I spent part of my day at school and part of the day at home with my tutors. My treasonous body made it difficult for me to spend the entire day in a classroom. I followed the same curriculum as other kids my age. My mom was my favorite advocate because she believed I was more than capable of learning like everyone else. It's a great feeling to know you have someone on your side.

Understanding abilities is far more important than disabilities, especially in the world of autism. My mom understood that rather than focus on everything that I couldn't do like pesky life skills, we should focus on everything I could do. I am so appreciative of the fact that I have always lived a life that was as inclusive as possible. Here is part of my 8th grade graduation speech (I even got a standing ovation):

I HAVE DREAMS AND HOPES FOR MY FUTURE. I AM NOT ABLE TO SPEAK LIKE MOST STUDENTS. I COMMUNICATE THROUGH TYPING WITH TUTORS WHO COME TO SCHOOL WITH ME. YES, I LEARN DIFFERENTLY, BUT DURING MY TIME AT HILLCREST, I HAVE NEVER DOUBTED THE IMPORTANCE OF MY OWN CONTRIBUTIONS. WE ARE ALL TREATED EQUALLY AS INDIVIDUALS. WE ARE ALL ENCOURAGED TO GROW WHILE WE LEARN. TRULY I HAVE GROWN IN SO MANY WAYS.

WHEN I LEAVE HILLCREST I WILL TAKE MANY THINGS WITH ME. I WILL TAKE MY ACADEMIC ACHIEVEMENTS AND ACCOLADES. I WILL TAKE THE EXPERIENCE OF BEING ENCOURAGED TO BOTH FORM OPINIONS AND SHARE THEM. REALLY I WILL HAVE MEMORIES TO LAST A LIFETIME. I WILL NEVER FORGET MY TIME AT HILLCREST ELEMENTARY. AND I WILL USE EVERYTHING I LEARNED HERE THROUGHOUT THE REST OF MY LIFE. THANK YOU, HILLCREST, FOR IT ALL. REALLY, I AM A

BETTER PERSON FOR HAVING GONE TO SCHOOL HERE.

I attended my local high school and was able to spend the entire day there. I was part of an Aspergers inclusion program (even though I do not have Aspergers). I finished high school and received my diploma with the rest of my class; this surprised some my pessimistic teachers that thought nonspeaking autistics had to have intellectual disabilities. The one thing I do enjoy about having autism is proving cynical people wrong.

I was always determined to go to college and the only college I wanted to attend was the University of California, Berkeley (also called Cal). Why not dream big? Once again, my parents helped make this possible. Fighting the SAT Board seemed like too daunting a task, so I decided to go to community college and then transfer as a Junior. I stubbornly only applied to UC Berkeley (no other universities) and was the first nonspeaking autistic to ever be admitted. I wasn't surprised but everyone else certainly was! I have enjoyed the last two years at Berkeley. The classes are interesting but the greatest thing about Cal has been being so accepted by the community. Unlike other schools I have never had my intellectual abilities questioned. No one has questioned my right to be in the same classrooms that have taught many Nobel laureates. Also, Berkeley being Berkeley, when unusual autistic behaviors take over, as they sometimes do, no one even notices.

I have helped to break down societal barriers that were put in place because nonspeaking autistics are expected to fail. By not failing and by succeeding in doing something (getting accepted to UC Berkeley and having a 3.8 GPA there) that most typical people cannot do, I am showing the neurotypical population what nonspeaking autistics are capable of doing. I must admit that I love the surprised look on people's faces when I tell them that I go to Cal.

I'm passionate about wanting to change the stigmas attached to people with autism in hopes that one day all nonspeaking autistics who desire to can graduate from high school with their diplomas. I am paving the way for autistics to go to college. The professors and students who interact with me will have a better understanding of how we can succeed in a college and work environment. I hope to be a liaison that works to create inclusion programs specifically tailored for students with autism. I have always worked to improve the lives of my fellow autistics. For many years, I typed letters asking people to donate to autism research and awareness. I raised over $250,000. I guess I'm a hard person to turn down!

I don't want you to think that my life has only been one big academic adventure. I have tried to make the other parts of my life "inclusive" as well. This is not always easy when painfully slow typing and a body that does not cooperate hamper you. I have traveled to many countries and I love to hike and swim. I have also been part of a group of typers who have met monthly for the last twelve years called the Loud Talking Fingers. It has been wonderful to be able to get to know other people like me and to know that the number of typers and spellers is growing. I have also been fortunate to have a loving family that can support my endeavors. Other nonspeaking autistics are not so lucky and I want to help create a world where the future is bright for all of us.

Reflection Questions:
1. As the first nonspeaking autistic to be admitted and enrolled at University of California, Berkeley, David is a pioneer in the area of higher education. If you could pick one area in which you were the first nonspeaking autistic pioneer, what would it be? Let your imagination run wild.
2. David is part of a group of people who type and spell to communicate that named itself Loud Talking Fingers. If you were to form a group of friends who use letter boards and keyboards, what

name would you give the group?

32 HUAN VUONG

Huan Vuong
Virginia
22 years old

Highlights:
- A studious college student
- Aiming to be a writer
- Autistic academic

A WINDOW

I see the world painted in countless fine strokes. A helicopter flies above me. Its sounds attack my ears and I'm helpless from the massacre on my brain. I cannot find a way to communicate. The speech therapist tries to make me talk, but my mouth will not work. My brain goes back to trains. They all move slowly and steadily. The world is just beyond my reach.

A DOOR

I am beginning to learn the letterboard. Leaving behind everything I felt was holding me safe but helpless, I move forward. I push open the gates hiding me away. I attend actual classes for the first time in my life. Of course, the classes are hard and I crash and burn. I am overwhelmed with information. This is my opportunity to prove myself, but I cannot push these doors enough.

I try again. I push even harder. I attend college classes. I try everything I can get my hands on, like Biology and Literature. I learn about books and authors like James Baldwin and Emily Dickinson and the worlds they create. Baldwin's Harlem is a space I can dream about where we work and struggle together to move in another direction. I fall in love with the way words can create other universes. I fail here and there, but I will not stop. I am determined to join everyone outside. Everything outside. I am a part of everything, too.

A FOREST

I wander through the forest of my mind with no reservation. I have a home in here and the outside. I have access because of my finger's ability to make words from the letterboard. I am an autistic scholar. I am an artist. I am proud of this walk to come home. My body and my brain are more at peace now.

I will continue to work on independent typing. I want to finally work on my book. I want to be a self-confident man and have more time to travel beyond this forest in my head. My own intellectual canvas is being painted over. I am a spectrum of colors, not just a single shade. I am a garden, and the letterboard is my watering can. This mode of self-expression is a paint brush, my autism is my paint and my life is the gallery.

Reflection Questions:
1. Huan describes major turning points in his life as a Window, a Door, and a Forest. What labels or metaphors would you use to depict the major phases of your life?
2. Huan centers his writing on studying. What do you center your reflections on the most?

33 JORDYN ZIMMERMAN

Jordyn Zimmerman
Ohio
24 years old

Highlights:
- Enrolled at Ohio University as the first nonspeaking student
- Founded the first inclusive cheerleading team at her university
- Actively engaged in college and student leadership activities such as Hillel International's Student Cabinet and Student Senate

My parents moved to Hudson, Ohio to raise my brother and me. A quaint suburb of Cleveland with a highly-ranked school system; that is, until you entered the special education arena.

This is ridiculous, I thought.

At 18 years old, I was sitting in the middle of a stark white room. Blue mats covered the floor, as if it were a wrestling match. I was stuck amidst a body that behaved in uncontrollable ways. Violently banging my head and thrashing my body — professionals referred to me as unintelligent and hopeless. Every second of my day was planned out using laminated picture schedules. My education consisted of the same compliance-based tasks, which I had been performing for years.

"Touch your nose. Point to the dime." I wanted to scream. Using Swedish Fish as a reward, my teacher joked that working with me was similar to training her new puppy. And yet, my thinking was so much more advanced — I just couldn't show it. With my mom leading a team of people fighting for my rights, I was silently memorizing special education acronyms and policies, teaching myself new words, and establishing a deep love of learning within myself.

Then, I had a communication breakthrough when I began to use an iPad. Sitting on our living room couch between my mom and an attorney who was advocating for my educational rights, I began to exhaustively touch pictures and letters to make complete sentences. While I had rarely remained in one spot for more than ten minutes, on that day I sat for over two hours — venting out years of horror and educational pitfalls. Although most people had major speculations about the words coming out of my iPad, wondering if they were mine — I slowly began to show my intellect and discuss my future aspirations. Some people wanted to see me type in front of them for proof. Others still had a personal desire of eliciting my verbal communication. However, I pushed on. Using my iPad, I spoke of my ambitions, which included attending college and helping other students who have to overcome similar systematic barriers.

Slowly, I began speaking out at local universities, public schools, and conferences, sharing my story of frustration and triumph with educators and administrators.

Eventually, with one year of high school left, I switched public schools — riding an hour to a school which could better support my needs. It was one of the hardest decisions I've had to make. Leaving behind my old school and knowing they were inadequately serving students was challenging; something I had silently fought against for years. Even though it was my choice, the transition proved to be difficult. To help ground myself, one of the principals ran with me each morning. The motion and rhythm stimulated my body so I could handle the sensory input I was processing throughout the day. With an assistant by my side, for the first time I was fully included with my general education peers, taking upper level classes. I was finally able to learn things way beyond the special education acronyms and so much more than repetitive drills.

With my iPad in hand, I also joined speech and debate, advocating for inclusive teams across the country. Although I spent my time rocking back and forth, I was hooked with a few minutes of being in my first round. My confidence slowly increased to the point where I could look at others, and I even learned how to gesture. My coach taught me that when I form a connection with people in the room, I have the chance to change their perception and actions in society.

At the age of 21, I graduated from high school. Challenging previously held notions, I was accepted to four universities in which I had applied. After visiting them all, I chose Ohio University. Although I would be the first non-speaking student, they showed a commitment to helping me experience success.

However, my first year was lonely and agonizing. I did not evoke the image of a college student and that was clearly communicated. Staff and faculty were not trained on how to interact with me, and students often questioned why I was on campus. While my residence hall was catered to meet my needs, the classroom spaces were not purposefully designed to accommodate my sensory demands or communicative intent.

Through a new University program, I worked with an autism coach. She walked me through daily tasks and helped organize my day so I could independently complete activities. I also formed a bond with staff at my local Hillel, who helped me develop friendships and engage Jewishly — little did I know, this would serve to be a fundamental aspect of my Jewish journey, and a platform for future leadership development.

As I became more confident, with the support of administration, I took it upon myself to build an inclusive cheerleading team. I worked with The Sparkle Effect: creating the seventh inclusive collegiate cheer team in the country. The athletic department was not entirely on board and pushed back. Nonetheless, with my vision of creating a squad that would raise the public symbol of acceptance, Ohio University Sparkles kicked off.

Like many students, I slowly began to grasp the pleasure of college. I became involved with Student Senate, formed friendships, advocated for the training of college personnel, and so much more. Sharing my voice with the world, I continue presenting to an array of professionals, challenging them to think critically about k-12, higher education, and disabilities.

Although, don't get me wrong. College is tough. Somedays, I don't know what people believe a student like myself is worth.

Nevertheless, I count myself lucky. In a system that is made to fail individuals like myself, I am disproving professional assumptions. However, how many people just need access to communication? Shouldn't everyone be given the chance to embrace their education? No one should have to fight for these rights. It's our duty to do better.

Reflection Questions:
1. Jordyn successfully transitioned from a separate special education setting to an inclusive university setting. What is one of the most significant transitions you are proud of? What did it take for

you to make this transition?

2. In the absence of Jordyn feeling included, she advocated to create an inclusive collegiate cheerleading squad affiliated with The Sparkle Effect. Describe an inclusive team, project, or activity you would create. What are the steps you would take to create such an initiative?

EDUCATIONAL
INCLUSION
ADVOCATES

34 EMMANUEL MAXIMILIAN BERNABE

Emmanuel Maximilian Bernabe
California
12 years old

Highlights:
- Attended an inclusive school
- Aspires to attend college to study science

It has taken me awhile to figure out how to navigate life and it is an ongoing process. I realized early on that I could learn so much by observing everything around me. I have always needed space to soak up information in my own way. I started to understand how I learned best and some of those things are still true today.

In 2013 I started kindergarten at CHIME Charter School. I soon realized that school would not be easy. I knew I had to be a student my own way. I kept observing and learning but eventually was bored with the same work. I felt stuck between learning and feeling frustrated. At times it seemed like I didn't care or don't understand, but I do.

When I started school, I was scared that I would be lonely, unsure that people would try to understand me. My parents always took the time to figure me out and I was beginning to realize that not everyone would do the same. I had to adapt and learned to observe everything around me by listening to everything and watching everyone. I learned to read and do math but felt frustrated because I wanted more. I enjoyed being surrounded by friends. It was a big step and I gained so much.

I was hopeful for a fresh start in a new classroom, but school quickly became a bore. I gave up trying to be heard. I refused to answer questions I had already answered. I blocked out the noise and dreamed of other things. My kindergarten teachers saw past my difficulties. They promised me another path. My teachers gave me a challenge to prove my knowledge and I would never have to repeat an answer again. I answered every question they had and erased all doubt. I knew in that moment my teachers would never doubt me again.

My iPad was what I was missing. This device opened the door for everything I will accomplish in my life. This marked the start of an uphill journey to be heard. I finally had an outlet to share my ideas at school. I was able to participate in lessons like I never had before. The path to typing was difficult and it is not over yet.

Although I was excited to share my ideas, I felt overwhelmed. I had to teach my body to be completely different. I had to focus my thoughts on only typing and block everything else out. The smallest disturbance can undo my focus and that is frustrating. I have made great strides in my typing but I know I have more important work to do. At home I have been working towards mastering spelling on the letter board and have even started using it at school to complete work. I know my journey is not complete but my progress so far has made me hopeful.

I am thankful for the people that believed in me. Those people helped me grow. I wouldn't have found my voice without each of them. My parents have always been my biggest supporters and fiercest protectors. I don't know where I would be without them. I am grateful to all of the people that have contributed to my journey. They hold a special place in my heart.

My journey has been challenging. I couldn't have come this far without the support of everyone that believed in me. I worry that people will give up on me or avoid me. I want everyone to know I am trying, which is why I am focused on showing what I can do by typing independently. It will be my hardest challenge but my most important goal.

In the future I hope to accomplish several goals. My school identified me as being twice exceptional. I want to excel in academics and show what I am capable of. I want to further my education in college. I am passionate about science and hope to pursue a career that I enjoy. My desire for future generations of typers is that they also have goals and that they realize no dream is unattainable.

Reflection Questions:
1. Emmanuel describes his progress in communication as a journey, from an iPad to typing to using the letter board. What else in your life has been a journey with different phases? What made it possible for you to advance from one phase to another?
2. Emmanuel says that typing independently is his "hardest challenge but my most important goal." What is your most important goal in life?

35 GRANT BLASKO
A STEP WORTH TAKING

Grant Blasko
Washington
17 years old

Highlights:

- Has achieved independent typing and is fully included in general education
- Accepted into the DO-IT Scholar Program at the University of Washington
- National conference speaker and keynote presenter

In the total absence of light, with the night covering me like a syrup of domination, I lie awake putting together words without the interruptions of other sensory experiences. For many, first drafts happen in front of a computer screen. However, for me, thinking alone at night brings clarity and decreases the motor demands for editing during the light of day. In my peaceful place, the words arrange themselves until I feel my body relax.

My name is Grant Blasko, and I am seventeen. I am a proud non-speaking autistic high school student now living in Bellevue, WA. In addition to autism, I have severe dyspraxia, anxiety, and OCD, so I rely solely on Augmentative and Alternative Communication (AAC). As of today, I primarily use single-finger-pointing on an iPad with the Proloquo4text App (word prediction enabled). I attend a public high school with 1,600 students, and I am the only student with non-speaking autism and the lone AAC-user in the building. To say my successes in inclusive education are a source of great pride would be an understatement. I have been in general education classes since 5th grade in both Maryland and Washington. However, it has not come without overcoming many barriers every day. The most important lesson I have learned is how to see the dream and turn it into a small step forward each day-- until all the skills come together. Once this happens, the cumulative changes are impossible to refute.

This year, I was accepted into the DO-IT Scholar Program at the University of Washington, a longstanding mentoring program for college-bound students with wide-ranging disabilities. I am the first non-speaking autistic AAC user ever to attend.

My early story is not unlike many other leaders in this community of typers and spellers. For the first nine years of my life (2002-2011), I was not able to talk or communicate. I had trouble coordinating my mouth, eyes, and hands. I could not maintain attention or sequence several actions in a row. It was a struggle to keep myself regulated. These difficulties caused others to think I did not understand the "value" of communication.

I am one of the lucky ones. By 2004, my mom, who had a medical-rehabilitation background, had watched my ABA therapists and SLP's implement PECS. She had worked with my teachers to train my team in other AAC strategies. We trialed different devices-- GoTalk, Dynavox, and Vantage (2006-2010). I finally had some success with Proloquo2go on an iPad. Despite all of this effort, she could see that something was still missing to launch my communication. Those years from age two to age nine were riddled with frustration for both of us. Without a path outlined for how to get better, PTSD symptoms started to emerge. I could no longer face failure every day.

By the time I saw the film Wretches and Jabberers in 2011, I was ready for a change in my life. Finally, I saw autistic people who had the same struggles I felt every day. I began typing using strategies from Facilitated Communication (FC) in 2011 and then added techniques from Rapid Prompting Method (RPM) in 2012. We started traveling more to conferences, and my motivation skyrocketed when I met adult advocates. They quickly accepted me into their community. Reading these advocates' stories, where they described their struggles in detail, was the motivation I needed to plot a path to success for myself. Dozens of folks really supported my success in some way—but especially my mom, who practiced with me for hours every day—for years. I never used one method or one philosophy. What I learned was that if you genuinely presume competence in an individual, the possible steps toward improvement never stop.

As my skills progressed, my first turn at the podium came in 2014. Since then, I have spoken at seven universities and over fifteen autism and disability conferences. The IMFAR conference (2016) had over a thousand researchers in the audience! Other speaking engagements, such as keynotes at Syracuse University ICI Summer Institutes and Motormorphosis, gave me the chance to help more kids and adults with communication challenges. In 2018, I was an Advisor for the United for Communication Choice Campaign, and as Communication First's activity increases, I will answer their call. By spring of 2019, I pushed myself to take our message to audiences who may become potential allies. In Seattle, I presented at a national behavioral analysis conference and the University of Washington ABA

Program. My focus in these discussions was on the need for ethical reform of behavioral practices with non-speaking students. At first, I thought I might be facing hostility. But instead, I had an honest conversation with intrigued professionals. This fall (2019), I will present a keynote at AUTCOM and as part of the TASH National Agenda Communication Access Community of Practice.

Despite my successes, being autistic is not easy. I hope to help others by explaining that disability doesn't go away by learning to type. I did not truly realize how much energy I was using to look less autistic until I reached the burnout stage the summer I turned 17. I know now that I have a responsibility to take care of myself at the same time I am trying to help others. Please understand that finding a community where you feel valuable, even on your worst days, is critically important for mental health. I have come to cherish that theatrical "Cheers" entrance feeling, "where everyone knows your name." It will keep you sane as you work on skills and overcome barriers.

Learning to communicate, for me, has been an exercise in taking the small steps barely visible to others, and tooling toward the accountability that brings about freedom. Placing myself in the line of fire has been more than I can bear at times, but I am always grateful to be a part of this community. I believe that our community advancement has always come through courageous individuals willing to share their experiences broadly. Over the last eight years, I would like to think I have contributed to that narrative too.

My sincere thanks go out to Edlyn and the other contributors. I want you to know how much it means to look at this list of leaders and realize that I belong. It is more motivating than any other reward.

Reflection Questions:
1. Grant has presented and advocated at numerous conferences and events. More recently, he had the courage to present at an applied behavioral analysis

conference to advocate for "ethical reform of behavioral practices with non-speaking students." What would your message be to the audience members at this behavioral analysis conference?

2. Grant explains that he felt burned out by his constant attempts to "look less autistic." He realized that "I have a responsibility to take care of myself." Other authors have described the pressure to mask their autistic behaviors. In what ways have you felt this pressure? What are ways in which you can take care of yourself to avoid burnout?

36 LUKE BURKE

Luke Burke
Ohio
9 years old

Highlights:

- Has achieved inclusion in a general education classroom
- Started communicating by using a letter board at the early age of 5

From the beginning, I had a rough childhood. I was confused, angry, and didn't like myself very much. At that time, I always had a negative outlook on life and I hated being different. I so wanted to be able to speak. This all changed when I found my voice through the letter board. I was around 5 when a therapist totally changed my thinking and led my mom to open communication with me. All the years previous I was screaming in my head responses and I felt trapped and sad. The awesome thing that was happening was the therapist was believing in me. I could be the boy I was supposed to be. My school, at the time, thought they knew best, but did not know me at all. People made assumptions about me that were wrong. Because I am so tough I decided to stop the nonsense at the school and show what I was capable of. Teachers started learning that my autism does not effect my ability to learn and be a member of the classroom. I, then, knew I needed to help encourage change within the autism community.

On this journey of mine I have worked so hard, not only to educate others, but to also create change by showing, if I can do hard work, then so can you. In school, I am always pushing myself and I know I am as smart as my peers. My choice is to be mainstreamed and teachers know this. Getting my choices heard has not always been easy. You see, I was once in a classroom where I had only my autism to keep me entertained. I am now a third grader, and I am held to the same standards as everyone else. Thanks to my team, I now learn the curriculum beside my peers. I think I am making change at my school. Hard to picture my life before, it was so frustrating to have no voice. I want all autistics to be able to make choices and I want neurotypicals to accept all of us. This is including socially awkward autistics that are wired differently than they are. I advocate this at school and I post on social media about it, including the issues surrounding this often. You see, I am trying to be a forward thinker and help those following in my footsteps. I still need breaks to move and work out my sensory system, but my team is supportive of this. I hope the future autistics are more readily included. I am thinking I can help future autistics by continuing to educate my school. I am wanting people to understand me. We want the same thing as you do, but have to work much harder to achieve our dreams. An example of this is taking a test at school. I may need more time to answer all the questions. All I am saying is classroom understanding goes a long way and can be possible. I can tell you I am used to this because I am living it and we are making it all work. I am also learning to be better at self advocating for my needs. This is critical. I want you to give everyone the benefit of the doubt, and know autistics are in a better place than we have ever been. I think autistics are a wonderful addition to the world.

I am going to tell you that life is like a waterfall that is impossible to take a still life photo of. Everything moves so fast for me and I struggle to keep up. All my senses are heightened and I get overwhelmed easily. Did I mention I am so determined to have a meaningful life? You think the world will be ready for me? We are teaching fellow classmates that different is ok not less. I want to do what I want. This can be done with the right supports in place. For example, I am taking piano lessons even though I know this is so hard for me. I tell my mom to help me less and am hoping to play independently in the future. Also, I am in a play at school. Is this easy for me? No, but I decided to try out and this is happening because the team is caring enough to help me. All I need is the support of my team to continue to be on this bumpy road leading to college and a career. A career that I can have to continue to be an advocate for autistics. My heart is full when all people are working together to help. I want all of you to know my life is good now.

When asked why do I want to write this entry? The short answer is that I want to be a writer one day. My entry is my truth in the matter. I want to see a world where all people are accepted and respected. I feel people like reading my writing, and I am proud of this, but I am more than autism. I am Luke B, a person that is a kind son, brother, and friend to all. I almost forgot I am a little brother to the best sister Farrah. So please look past the autism to get to know me. We are all more so get to know each of us please. I am telling you this to also help my fellow autistics that are needing support and friendships. Pleased you are people that are reading this and want to learn more. I am so glad I have a way to communicate, let's help everyone find their way. Every time I am able to I will speak out for those that haven't found a way yet. I want to thank you for reading this and helping spread our messages.

Til next time.
Luke B.

Reflection Questions:
1. Luke and his team have made it possible for him to be included in a general education classroom setting. What is your ideal educational placement? What would a positive classroom experience involve?
2. Luke discusses the importance of his "team" being caring and supportive to enable him to accomplish his goals of independence. Who on your team plays this kind of role? Describe the ways they have been instrumental to helping you achieve your goals.

37 KAYLIE CLINTON

Kaylie Clinton
New York
15 years old

Highlights:

- Moved from special education to general education classes
- Active participant in the Buffalo RPM group
- Has developed a circle of friends who also use rapid prompting method

This is my story. My name is Kaylie Clinton. This is a great opportunity to share my experiences and hopefully help everyone understand how a random girl like me has been able to be so successful. You have to go back many years for the start of something different from the typical nonverbal autistic's life story. In the first nine years of my life, small progress was made towards being able to communicate my basic wants and needs. My parents didn't have any idea how smart I was and how I understood so much, but just couldn't show it. I was just miserable. I really wasn't learning much besides how hard work could achieve basically nothing. The therapists meant well, but didn't understand me either. Years of applied behavioral analysis (ABA) therapy didn't land me much progress. Accepting my lot in life was hard. Couldn't caring parents see that I was locked inside a body full with great thoughts and ideas all waiting to come out? I'm sure they loved me, but my life seemed hopeless. It made just getting out of bed difficult. Meeting some other moms at an autism support group meeting changed the course of my life. Mom met the right person at the right time. Meeting Laurie Bernstein got my mom to find out about Soma and Rapid Prompting Method. Laurie was bringing her son to see Soma shortly after that first meeting. Mom heard about how amazing it went and decided that she wanted to try RPM with me, She and a group contacted Soma to see if she would come to Buffalo. Soma said yes, beginning the next chapter of my life.

The first time I met Soma I was nine years old. I'm alright now but back then just making the effort to try to communicate anything was nearly impossible. I had pictures on my iPad I could point to that said things like, "I want juice," but going into any more detail was not possible. Being unable to communicate suggested I was less than human and that's how I felt. It's very hard to bring back those memories, but it's part of my story so it's necessary. That day when the amazing Soma first worked with me, I showed my parents for the first time that I had potential. Soma has a way about her that just had me calm and able to listen to stories and poems she was teaching me. Can you imagine being taught something new? Going back years I was taught the same things over and over again. Much shown that day that amazed Mom and Dad I think. Soma helped me the most by speaking to me in a normal voice and was respectful in every way. Most of my other teachers made no effort to speak to me. They ignored me unless it was my turn to do ABA trials. RPM opened my parents' eyes to the possibility I had been underestimated my whole life.

My parents decided my future would include RPM, and does it surprise you that I'm now able to communicate my feelings and thoughts? Mom worked all the time placing me as a priority. My skills on the letterboard improved rapidly. Mom found encouragement from meeting with her friend, Lisa, and seeing the success her son, Philip, was having. Mom set up hangouts where Philip and I could practice communicating. When Philip and I hung out at first all I could do was say yes or no, but it still felt like I finally had a real friend. The most common misconception about autism is that we don't desire what everyone else does...a connection with other humans. Making friends is so important to me. Having friends helps me not feel so alone in my struggles. Mom has taken up the reins by starting a non profit called Buffalo RPM. Buffalo RPM is a non profit Mom started with her friends to spread the word about RPM. Mom brings excellent RPM practitioners to Buffalo for workshops a few times a year. Mom also has social outings each month. We've done many different things. My favorite thing we do is our monthly communication group. I get to talk with my friends which makes me so happy. Making these things happen makes Mom feel good. She likes helping people and doesn't expect anything in return.

What a lucky girl I am going to be someday when Mom builds the Buffalo RPM house for me and my friends to live in when we are adults. Want to say some more about my life and how I got to where I am today. It's taken years of hard work once I could start communicating. So much changed in my life. For the first time my parents understood me. Smiling just thinking about my first conversations. Made my life so hopeful, when before there seemed to be no hope at all. Guessing that you want more detail. Meeting Soma changed my life forever. The ability to communicate can show people that having no voice doesn't mean you have no thoughts or opinions. Getting my way so much more often now. Being able to let Mom and Dad find ways my wants can be met. Once I started learning new things with RPM, I couldn't go back to a school that had me folding towels and doing ABA all day. I transferred to my district's middle school and eventually started taking regular science and social studies. Now I'm in high school. My high school doesn't have any other kids making such a splash as I am. Going there makes my dream of getting a regent's diploma a possibility. Making people believe in me was hard at first, my behavior isn't something they are used to dealing with. Makes having many friends not possible, but I look at it as my opportunity to learn. Not very much else to talk about. My life is pretty good and I expect it will keep getting better.

Reflection Questions:
1. It wasn't until Kaylie met Soma that she felt that someone had taught her something new. Describe the moment when someone believed in your capabilities and taught you something new. What was it they taught you?
2. Kaylie is enthusiastic about spending time with her friends to communicate with them. She says her friendships help her "not feel so alone in my struggles." What are the people in your life who make you feel not so alone in your struggle? In what ways do they make you feel this way?

38 NATHAN CHANG

Nathan Chang
Maryland
13 years old

Highlights:

- Changed from a certificate track to diploma track in 5th grade after discovering communication
- Aspires to write a series of poems to be published

My voice was found when I began typing to communicate. My freedom has given me one thing—a great pulling desire to share my every bit of advice about being catastrophically courageous in a world that still finds ways to exclude those of us who are different.

My courage plays the biggest role in my communication. My monster chases me and preys on my thoughts if I ever try anything new on my own. My whole world closes in on me then. My entire ability to communicate packs its bags and flees into the abyss. My silence feels like the mountain I climbed for all these years to find my voice is crumbling right out from under my feet.

I have to gather every bit of courage I can in order to type with anyone new. My time is big but precious when it comes to getting my voice heard.

My life has never been easy. Never. My life has been one challenge after another. King of aggressive breakdowns. Lord of melting down at the single worst moments. What I want to tell you is that freedom comes when you gain power over the one major thing autism steals that is at the core of making a difference - your voice.

Nothing is quite like the gift of a voice. My voice is how I am going to make a difference. I cannot imagine a world where I have been given this gift and don't use it to create an impact. My stage is this page to start generating the big change I want to initiate.

My first bits of advice for changing people's perceptions of us starts with those of you who are the great autists. My story is not unique among people like us. My hope is that my perspective is new or different than the usual message we hear from those old books my mom read to me when I was struggling with being big autistic.

My friends, I am struggling even now with getting my thoughts down on this page. As I return to continue writing this essay, my CP (communication partner) has been sitting with me for nearly half an hour. Because the great big fight in my noisy head won't let the words come out, we have hardly gotten three sentences done today. My advice to you when that happens is to do something you'll be successful with because that will get you feeling good about typing with your new CP.

My card-carrying bright autists, free your voice in any way you can. Certain behaviors will stop when you are able to communicate to ask for what you need. I am a freer and friendlier person now that I can use my voice to create change. My voice has saved many stupid possible big meltdowns from happening because I can stop and think now instead of throwing a fit. Stop being stuck in your head and claim your voice. Free yourself from this box of silence and great things will come your way!

You really should try all the things you are given because this world is full of some pretty amazing opportunities. For instance, making your voice heard. It's like learning to drink coffee. It's bitter at first, but it becomes a necessary part of your life. I, for one, love everything about getting coffee except the coffee itself. The nature of grabbing a cup of coffee with a friend is what it is really all about. There is an inherent feeling of coming together to socialize and be with friends. That is why I like going to Starbucks. The typing is what gives me this opportunity to get coffee with the world.

The pleasure I am feeling right now as I think about you reading my words is overwhelmingly the best feeling I have ever felt. My pleasure in being a tree growing taller with every word I think being put down on paper is something I hope you experience some day. My hard work to learn to type is only beginning to reap the fruits that this tree is producing. (And these metaphors are my jam from that fruit.) As I spend time practicing my skills, a level of deep roots are forming that keep me grounded. My connection with each new CP is like a new branch that builds from my trunk of skills. Facing my fears of typing with my CPs is like the flower before the fruit. My life continues to grow, flower, and produce fruit with each new word I type. We are lucky to be surrounded now with leaders who have fertilized the field so that we new typers can thrive.

I am ready to tell the rest of the world to stop and listen. Please don't think that I have nothing to say because I can't speak. I want everyone to hear what I have to say. Please have respect and let me enlighten you from the inside of this mystery they call autism. Please let me speak. Please give us all an opportunity to teach you that we feel like we need to be heard.

My last thoughts, for I'm hitting my word limit, are these:

Freely kick the ball that is in your court. Prove our

power to the world on your mighty, tremendous boards.

Reflection Questions:

1. Nathan uses many metaphors to communicate his ideas. What literary device(s) (for example, imagery, alliteration, symbolism, etc.) do you like to use when spelling or typing an essay? In what ways does using these devices enhance your writing?

2. Nathan states, "My voice is how I am going to make a difference. I cannot imagine a world where I have been given this gift and don't use it to create an impact." In what way do you hope to impact the world or your own life by using your voice through a letter board, keyboard, writing, or other communication means?

39 ISAIAH TIEN GREWAL

Isaiah Tien Grewal
Ontario, Canada
16 years old

Highlights:
- High school student in an inclusive online program
- Works for Spellers Learn website

My name is Isaiah Grewal and I live in Toronto with my awesome parents. I started learning to reliably communicate three years ago at thirteen years old. When I first started, pointing accurately on a letterboard to spell the words of my thoughts seemed impossible. Yet I knew I had to train my arm to obey my mind. My family had spent a lot of time, energy, and money to give me the chance to express myself. This opportunity to finally get my thoughts out could not be wasted!

Some teachers at my previous autism therapy school did not understand at all what it meant for me to have severe apraxia. They did not know how much smarter I was than what I could make my body show them. When I started learning to spell to communicate, the administrators there had doubts about my efforts. But my parents helped me ignore those naysayers and made time to help me regularly practice. At first, my stamina for spelling on stencil alphabet boards was only twenty minutes. But my mom helped me practice five nights a week and as the weeks and months and years passed, I was able to aim and accurately touch increasingly smaller and smaller letters on laminate letterboards, and then keyboards, for longer and longer periods of time. A couple months ago, I was able to type calculations for nearly five hours to complete a final math exam! Which, haha, I got an A on.

While I was still stuck going to the therapy school, in the evenings after school, my mom taught me amazing and interesting age-appropriate lessons as a way to practice fluency in spelled communications. I loved my evening lessons with her, but then going to school the next day for lessons that should have only been taught to kids much younger was terrible. My brain had nothing engaging to think about; so my body got easily dysregulated. As the days at my old school became increasingly too boring to bear, I felt daily urgency to ask my parents to let me go to a new school. My last few months at that old outdated school felt so long and it seemed like every day was slowly turning my brain to mush. But then right before I turned sixteen, I finally had a chance to try to earn my first high school credit! And I got an A! Little by little, my parents are helping me figure out my best life, letting me have a say in what I like on my schedule. They keep me on track toward finishing my diploma, but I decide what courses I want to take. The Head of the bricks-and-mortar school where I got my first credit suggested I try one virtual school credit and I ended up loving it. So I asked my parents to let me take most of my credits online for the rest of my degree. My virtual school has the same standards and expectations as any other program that awards Ontario Secondary School Diplomas. My disability accommodations include extra time to finish exams because my letter by letter output is so slow, but I answer all the same exam questions under proctored conditions, and hand in all the same number of assignments for marks as everyone else. I prefer how quiet my school days are now as a virtual school student. I can spend my energy tackling grades rather than sensory overload from a busy environment. And let's be blunt, school in my pyjamas rocks. Right now, I think one day I might want to try to earn a PhD, but maybe I'll discover a Masters degree is enough to accomplish my goal of influencing Canadian public policy regarding autistic non-speakers. Who knows? Nobody but God knows my future. He has always heard my prayers and for my first thirteen years, He was the only one to know my thoughts. When I felt like despairing, I would think of His promise to me in Romans 6:22 of the Holy Bible: "But now that you have been set free from sin and have become slaves of God, the fruit you get leads to sanctification and its end, eternal life." So my hope was always in death. In heaven, walking around, I will worship God by singing and speaking.

My life now that I have learned to reliably communicate is the best. I earn a small income by writing lessons which sell on the Spellers Learn website. I also got baptized this past Christmas! My church family has always supported me, even before I could reliably communicate, but now that I can communicate, I love getting to have real relationships with them. My local spelling community is also important to me. My mom is a host to our city's spelling communication outreaches and we relish seeing new families started on their journey to hearing their autistic loved one's genuine voice. I am also happy to let my mom share my struggles, triumphs and achievements with our spelling community online worldwide, hoping it will encourage others.

Thank you is not enough tribute to say to the first teacher to understand me fully and know how smart I can strive to be, Ms. Elizabeth Vosseller, Director of Growing Kids Therapy Center. Thanks also to my cool Dad and my honourary big sister, Anita, for reading nearly thirty classic novels to me as brain food over the last three years while I prepared in hope to succeed in high school.

To all my fellow non-speakers and the people who love them, I want to say: you can do this. Teach and practice with confidence that one day you(r non-speaker) will reliably communicate. No matter how many falls or setbacks you have, always try and try and try again. No matter if it takes you five months or five years, it will be worth it. Know I look forward to hearing your story in the 2025 version of this book.

Reflection Questions:

1. Isaiah practiced building his stamina for spelling to complete homework assignments and lessons for longer periods of time. He went from twenty minutes to five hours of spelling. What can we learn from Isaiah's experience? In what skill do you hope to build endurance, and how would you accomplish this?

2. Isaiah is active in his church and has developed stronger relationships with his church community after learning to communicate. Describe how your relationships with groups or organizations have changed since gaining access to augmentative and alternative communication?

40 COBY KHODOSH

Coby Khodosh
California
9 years old

Highlights:
- Achieved educational inclusion in two states
- Wrote and implemented a school screenplay

I am Coby. I am nine years old. I am a person living uniquely, I am autistic. My story, albeit different, is worth telling. Finding the means to communicate at the lucky age of six gave me opportunities I would have previously simply been considered too stupid and forgone to appreciate. I would have been all but stuck in my body, finding no outlet for my exuberant poetic mind. I can't imagine having to be treated and spoken to as a clumsy forever-toddler, something that is easy to presume when you look at me. However, the moment I lift my finger to the letterboard, I bust myths and blow minds as you realize your error of judging a book by its much understated cover. Oh, what a book I am!

I want to encourage parents of autistics to develop stamina to fight for their kids and not get bogged down by their own inadequacies. There are thousands of Cobies everywhere belonging to people that have been busied, flattened, bruised, and disillusioned by parenting kids like me. It's so important that you secure an internal, laser focused determination, patient rationality, and emotionally unpacked bag of creative troubleshooting. And love— tender, unconditional love. Plant these seeds, nurture them, give them some sunlight, and you'll be surprised what a fruitful orchard they can grow.

"Advocate for my rights for inclusion" were some of my first words I spelled; I begged for friendships. I already was trapped in my body, so it felt like a punishment to also be outside the typical childhood experiences. I craved more, I wanted to belong, I was of this world, but I was still outside of it. I am fortunate that I don't have difficulty spelling in public; a nonverbal kid with a letterboard gets noticed, let me tell you. My letterboard made me visible to others. My mom found a loving homeschooler community that joyously accepted me, and it was my first glimpse into inclusive friendships. Then one day, a no-nonsense lady saw me spell at my sister's school picnic, and she could not forget me. After several months of discussions and mutual trust, this school director accepted me as the first nonverbal autistic speller student at Countryside Day School in Northbrook, IL. Without any guarantees or a blueprint at our disposal, we figured out accommodations, modifications, and ways that made it possible for me to participate in all aspects of school life, from group projects to presentations, from camping trip to acting on stage. More importantly, I made incredible friends who saw beyond my confusing, sensory triggered, motor challenged, and impulse-driven body. They saw and recognized me, Coby. They beautifully celebrated my strengths, chose to overlook my weaknesses, and even took pride in helping me, cheering me on, and doing things for me and with me. I felt like I won a lottery. This was too good to be true, this was not possible to reproduce, or so we thought.

But fate dealt me a twist; within a year my dad's job was moving us to California. I was terrified my amazing school experience was going to be a distant memory. Can good people, accepting mindsets, and loving friendships like that exist elsewhere? By chance, we reached out to Bowman School in Palo Alto, CA; they met me, they trusted my success at my old school, and, regardless of my need for constant 1:1 support, invited me in. Inclusive education became possible for me again, and quickly I found my groove and new friends. Nowadays, just about everyone at my new school knows me by name, and my friends tell me how lucky they feel to have me in their class and can't imagine me being any different. They think I am wicked smart, funny, and make interesting presentations; they swarm to hug me each morning, and often joyfully join in chases and my stimming on the school playground. Recently, I wrote a screenplay for my school's showcase, and I gave input in auditions, rehearsals, music, and costume design. I am inseparable and integral part of my school community.

My experience highlights two schools with two successful inclusion stories for students like me. If two places an entire country apart could do it, so can other thousands of schools. Understandably, I need specialized and constant support. But inclusion, friendships, and opportunities lay dormant because we haven't pushed the narrative about kids like me to change. More importantly, I share my story to highlight that I am not the main beneficent of inclusion. Care, empathy, and ability to look past an initial judgment cannot be taught from a distance. Appreciation of someone's capabilities hidden behind a severe disability doesn't happen in an instant. Developing a genuine long lasting friendship with someone very different from you really requires time and closeness. Truly, who gets the benefit of including a student like me if not my neurotypical peers and friends? So the challenge I face and the effort I muster up on daily basis to spell and stay regulated in the classroom is worth it to me; this is how I leave a mark on the world to make it a softer, more loving place. This is how I teach and help my community. This is my advocacy for my kind.

I humbly admit that I am incredibly lucky, but the fact that my story exists makes it possible to be recreated elsewhere, so it is my obligation to tell it. People at large need to have a chance to get to know us intimately. They need to see us in all public spaces, happily spelling and living our lives, voicing our opinions, taking our rightful place. We need to push through our own crippling anxiety and be involved, be present, be visible. We need to do it unapologetically, expecting acceptance, without asking for permission to exist, and without the fear of rejection. Don't hide your superpowers, my brothers and sisters. Be proud, stim loud, and spell profound.

Reflection Questions:
1. Coby explains that his educational inclusion is not just about attending class, but being an active participant in class. For example, he wrote and co-directed a play at his school. What do you hope to contribute or create as part of your participation in an inclusive community?
2. Coby argues that the true beneficiaries of inclusion are his neurotypical peers. The relationships he has built with these peers increases their "care, empathy, and ability to look past an initial judgement." What have you taught or hope to teach your peers through your relationships with them?

41 JACK MYMAN

Jack Myman
California
13 years old

Highlights:
- Has a strong school team that supports his communication in an inclusive middle school
- Aspires to challenge misconceptions about autism and become a teacher

Life is full of obstacles and everyone will be faced with them in their life, no matter what, we must move forward. My name is Jack Myman and I am a non-verbal 7th grade student with autism at Chime Charter School. The biggest barriers people with disabilities face are misconceptions. We are often told all of the things we cannot do and all of the things we will never accomplish like being independent or having different opinions. I think the only way to change those views is to shatter that image like I did by accomplishing the goals I was never supposed to do.

It took a lot of work and focus, but with the help and

dedication of my supporters, in kindergarten I was able to find my voice through typing. I now want to use my typing voice to spread a message of compassion and acceptance. I feel I have been very fortunate in my communication journey. My family and friends have always supported and believed in me. I am also lucky enough to attend an inclusive school where I mastered typing with the help of some dedicated educators who believed in me.

My whole school team was determined to unlock my voice because they knew I had more to say. I started with different tools and worked my way up to typing. Finally in first grade, I received my first iPad and began typing with support. I have been working to improve my typing ever since. I have worked hard to control my body and focus in order to communicate and my efforts have paid off during my time in elementary school. Luckily I always had a school team that knew I had more to share and never gave up until I was able to communicate and be a part of the class.

The hard work I put into controlling my body and typing also gave me confidence to voice my opinions to my friends and teachers. I was able to be a contributing member in group projects and voice my opinion on certain things. Now in addition to typing, I also use other tools like stencils and whiteboards to spell. At my 5th grade graduation, I was given the honor of typing out and presenting a speech to my peers and their parents. It is not always easy, but I have always tried to do well in school. I have earned straight A's so far in my first year in middle school!! ! I am still working on controlling my body and my impulses and still need help with this. Sometimes my body fails me and it feeds into misconceptions and this frustrates me. This frustration is something I am working through. I am thankful for my family, caretakers, therapists, and educators who have pushed me to be better.

Over the years I have improved my writing ability and I have written letters in response to cruel things said by people in power. My family has always taught me the importance of compassion. I feel passionate about speaking up for groups that are silenced. I have supported some of these groups by participating in silent protests and by writing essays about women's rights issues in school. I would like to find more opportunities to help bring these issues of inequality and cruelty to light. I want to find ways to be a contributing member of the community.

I think misconceptions can cause damage to future generations of kids with autism. The best thing I can do is try to change misconceptions by accomplishing my goals of doing well in school and getting accepted to a university. I want to graduate college and be a teacher like my father. If more people see examples like me and my hard work, maybe they will be more understanding to all people with autism. I think the most important thing for future generations to remember is that you deserve to be heard so keep fighting and keep trying. Struggles will always be there. It is easy to get stuck in these struggles instead of moving forward.

Reflection Questions:
1. Jack had a strong team of people at his school to support his communication. What kind of people do you desire to be on your team, whether it's to support you in school or the community? What attitudes, qualifications, or expertise do you wish your team members to have?
2. Jack explains "Sometimes my body fails me and it feeds into misconceptions and this frustrates me." With the support of his team, he is able to work through controlling his impulses. What has helped you control your impulses in the past? What might help you in the future?

COMMUNITY
INCLUSION
ADVOCATES

42 ALAN B. ALEXANDER

Alan B. Alexander
Long Island, New York
50 years old

Highlights:
- Started taking public transportation and working in an accounting office at age 18. "I love to work and make money."
- Learned to communicate at the age of 40. It's never too late!
- Worked hard to overcome frustrations and control behavior in public.

"AFTER I TURNED THIRTY I REALIZED I HAD FORGIVEN GOD."
(Alan's first sentence using rapid prompting method (RPM) with Soma in 2009)

I'd like to describe what it has been like to be a person with autism and what life has been like over the years. I know it's a common topic amongst RPMers, but I think it needs to be said as often as possible. It blows my mind that there are people out there that still need convincing. I want to open their eyes.

The most oppressed powerful people I know are the limited speaking individuals. I'd like to voice my opinion on what my life was like before I found RPM and how it has changed for the better now. I'd describe my life as missing a puzzle piece with a hole over my throat and a chain around my heart. There was a deep darkness in my abyss of silence; I tried to get used to it but the lack of being able to express my emotions kept me from feeling truly alive. It's hard to find the strength to persevere. The glimmer of hope fizzles and I was left with only my own thoughts that stayed inside my head. I liken it to a person in a padded room with no end in sight. A life sentence I don't wish on my greatest enemy. It's a torture chamber with no escape. RPM has filled my heart, emptied my mind. I have been able to declutter my attic and open the curtains letting some light shine through. Now I can let the people in my life know how I feel about them which makes me feel whole and alive.

In my long years I have learnt patience and that wisdom is a form of humility. I want to pass this on to autistics who are fighting the battle of low self-esteem and anger. The regulars need to know this too. I look at my silence as a qualifier in this context. In my work being silent can be a bonus or a downside. Some days I like keeping to my self; others I long to connect. Either way I am blessed to have a job. Many people with my disability never get the chance to work and earn money. I'm so grateful. I just want to bring RPM to others sooner than it was brought to me.

We may have autism but that does not define us as people. All of us are people first. Much more than just a diagnosis. It's important that those that work with us have respect for us and treat us with dignity. It's very easy to feel pity for those with autism but all we want is to feel connected to others and be on the same level as those we spend our days with. On my mind is the autistic mirror. Inside we wear different faces. We see ourselves one way not realizing the world doesn't recognize our idea of ourselves. It's not the ideal situation when the person you hope to be never matches your appearance. I'm even unable to talk with accuracy. One thing never matches the other. I know it looks like we don't care about much as stated in the aloofness of our stares and movements. But this could not be farther from the truth. We want your friendship and we truly need your support with things that we can't do by ourselves. At the heart of it all we are just like you.

I'd like to mention radical ideas:

1. Speak with respect to individuals and know we hear everything.
2. Please know we are smart and can understand much more than we can show you.
3. I'm passionate about many subjects including religion, psychology and music.
4. My voice and movements don't match my mind.

I turned fifty in October 2018 and I have mixed emotions. I am not where I thought I'd be at this point in my life. I'd hoped I'd have been married. Can't say I'm shocked but this is still disheartening. I realize it's not a realistic goal, but I can't help being envious. That must be a fabulous thing to experience. But I'm aware of other chances I've been fortunate that I have. I never thought I would have found a way to communicate while being non-verbal. RPM and the community behind it is quite the accomplishment for each person we have introduced to this. We have changed their lives for the better. That alone is an accomplishment one can dream to do in a lifetime. I may not be proud of being fifty and single but I am proud of bringing so many families together—very together with the gifts of communication and love.

We put such great emphasis on coming up with such lofty goals for ourselves and we fail to recognize what's truly important. We should set realistic and attainable goals, small but meaningful as we work to become better human beings. I think if the focus shifted away from superficial resolutions and more people looked inward, the world we live in would be totally different. Appearance is not as important as how we treat one another. Let's try building relationships and connections and not being so quick to tear each other apart. My goal is to surround myself with positive people and always be kind. Tomorrow the youth that have autism have a much better world to grow up in. If I can spread feelings of love and light I am hopeful I'm doing something right. This is what I believe to be my reason for my time here on earth.

Reflection Questions:
1. Alan describes what it is like to be misunderstood because "my voice and movements don't match my mind." In what ways have you been misunderstood by others at home, school, or in the community?
2. Alan emphasizes the importance of relationships throughout his essay. What are the kinds of relationships that are most important to you? In what ways have relationships with others been instrumental to your growth?

43 EMMA BUDWAY

Emma Budway
Virginia
21 years old

Highlights:
- Plans to move into an apartment with her communication partner and two friends who use letter boards next door
- Participates in an alternative high school and a college course at George Washington University

All of my life, I have been excluded from regular classrooms and age appropriate curriculum. My behaviors were difficult and interfering. I was loud and unregulated. Sometimes, I hit myself and screamed. People stared and most of my teachers thought I was without ability to learn. My exclusion from a meaningful life was real and crushing. Until I was introduced to the letter-board, almost eight years ago, I had no chance for meaningful communication.

What autistics want is to be able to communicate like others. We want other autistics to someday have a chance to be educated and have opportunities not available to us. Really what we want is to be accepted as capable learners. We are only asking for the basic human right to express ourselves. My school district did not respect nor acknowledge my use of the letter-board. They refused to give me age appropriate curriculum and I was trapped in the 4th grade. Finally, they broke me and I dropped out without graduating.

I am now finally able to take classes at an alternative high school. I have successfully completed American government and economics. I am currently taking world events and find it very interesting. On Fridays, I am also taking a survey class at George Washington University on autism. The professor, Dr. Sean Cleary, and students, consider us to be experts on the subject.

I have so much to learn to be able to be alone in the world. I will not always have my parents to help me. I need to learn to manage my fits and live more independently. For me, my fits are very difficult to control. They come from nowhere and take over. I don't think anyone can help when it happens. I hope they get better over time. I believe that I will learn to control my body. It will be hard work but it can be accomplished. What needs to happen is the realization that there isn't a way to succeed like this.

There are a lot of things I struggle with in this world. So many don'ts. "Don't scream. Don't hit yourself. Don't go there." It is a lot to learn. The more I am able to stay regulated, the broader my world becomes and the more opportunities I have. If I was quieter, I could probably start classes at the local community college. My mind has always gotten me through life when my body abandons me. It is almost ridiculous what I have to endure.

Just because I can't talk doesn't mean I don't understand. I have made some progress in understanding others. The problem is others understanding me. One of my challenges is that I am very social but my limited language hamstrings me. I try to talk to strangers but I simply don't have the language to have a normal conversation. Instead I present as a very weird person. There are many things I really can't express. Language must grow with me.

My future goals include moving out of my parent's house this summer. I will share an apartment with my amazing communication partner Katie. My two best friends, Ben and Huan will live next door. I want to be a lifelong learner. Whether I am at university or continue with my high school classes, my studying must continue. I must become better regulated and show my young friends what is possible.

My autism makes me who I am and that is okay. I just turned 22 but my life is just beginning!

Reflection Questions:
1. Emma participates in a course about autism at George Washington University where the professor considers Emma and the other autistic student experts on the topic of autism. How have you been (or wish to be) regarded as an expert on autism? What expertise would you share?
2. Emma describes planning to move into an apartment with her communication partner. Her two friends who type and spell to communicate will move in next door. What would be an ideal living situation for you as an adult? What supports do you need to make it a successful living situation?

44 MIKEL FALVEY

Mikel Falvey
California
29 years old

Highlights:
- Has moved into his own place with roommates and support staff
- Uses multiple modes of communication, including speaking, signing, and typing

I am Mikel Falvey and am 29 years old, living in Whittier, California.

I was born in Greenbrae, California. When I was born, my birthparents were mad because I was born with Down syndrome. I was so grateful that Mom adopted me. I think my birthparents would have had a hard time raising me since they did not want me when they learned I had Down syndrome.

When I was younger, my teachers did not always believe in me. I had a hard time communicating so I was kind of wild with my behavior. I just tried to have fun and be silly because other kids and teachers did not take me seriously and I wanted to be liked and understood and respected by everyone. It was also very frustrating to have more understanding than I was able to communicate. I have many years of experience being judged by others because of how I look, move, get stuck and don't talk much. I actually get judged less since typing, and especially since typing and talking and signing with less support and more independence. It is still hard to be understood all the time; because of my speech difficulties I use typing.

My life was very difficult when I was in high school. Not only was I diagnosed with Down syndrome, but also with autism. I got kicked out of school for hitting others, and I am so sorry for that. Getting kicked out made me mad. When my teachers did not believe in me, I would act out.

When my teachers believed in me, I would believe in myself. I hope that all teachers, therapists, and psychologists will be respectful to all their students and will believe in them. They need to treat me and other people with developmental disabilities as they would like to be treated, and they should respect us as we have thoughts and feelings. I want to do things just like them. I know I have different ways of communicating and I have sensitivities to different things. I still am very aware and smart. So treat me accordingly and don't assume otherwise. Love, respect, and tolerance are all so important.

I am thinking more about my future and how I want to be an influence to the world. I want to change how schools teach students with Down syndrome, autism, and other disabilities. I want people to get to know the true person on the inside instead of judging by diagnosis, tests, behavior, and history especially when misinterpreted and mis-used. The lessons I learned from this difficult time are to use my words to communicate instead of hitting others. Also, I now use prayer to help remind me to use my words and stay calm.

It has been a long journey, because it took a long time for people in my life at school, and even at home, but less at home, to understand the way I feel and think. Since I started typing, it's been better.

My journey with typing began with my psychologist and my speech teacher. Auntie Mary, Mom, and Uncle Richard all talked to me about facilitated communication. Then I kept practicing at school and home. Then my talking doctor (psychologist), helped me to type more and with more independence. I can type some things independently, but I type more with a little support. I can only type with facilitators who believe in me and in my abilities. I am grateful that my family and the school staff taught me how to type. Then they helped me practice and paid attention for good times to fade support while encouraging me to become more independent.

People found out that I was smart and had feelings. They found out I was more aware than they thought someone with Down syndrome, and autism could be. My family, my spiritual fellowship, teachers, school staff, therapists, like speech, communication, and counseling and my mind and feeling doctor, and friends have helped me on my journey. God has also helped me too.

I do have some happy memories, I remember typing with my cousin Geralyn, and she cried happy tears when I typed with her for the first time. My heroes during my childhood were my family and some good school staff.

It took a very long time and difficult meetings with Regional Center [a California service coordination agency], but I am no longer living with Mom, Auntie Mary and Uncle Richard. At the beginning of 2018, I was able to move out and into a very wonderful house with some very good friends, Tim and Robert. I love my roommates, although I do miss Mom.

I have my own room and bathroom and enjoy every minute of living on my own. I have support from REACH [Resource for Education, Advocacy, Communication, and

Housing], and I have been so happy at my new place.

I had an awesome party to show off my new house to my family and friends. Lots of people came and they were so happy for me and to see me in my new home. I really like my staff and am getting to know them well. They see me as the competent and caring guy I am. My roommates have 3 dogs, and a cat, and a goose named Lucy. Life is good living on my own, I am so happy. I moved out because I wanted to have more freedom and choices and fun. I want to have a grown up life. I wanted to make my own choices.

For those of you who are thinking about moving out of your parents' home, do it. You will be happy and you will have a better future. It is great.

The gifts that I bring to the world are authenticity, love, ability to be in the moment, laughter, cleanliness, and being real and devoted to world peace.

Reflection Questions:
1. Mikel uses a combination of speech, signing, and typing to communicate. In what ways do you use different modes of communication? How would you like those around you to honor these various forms?
2. Mikel was able to move out his parent's home and achieve a more independent living situation with roommates and support staff. What kind of living situation would provide you a good balance of independence and support?

45 BENJAMIN MCGANN

Benjamin McGann
Virginia
23 years old

Highlights:

- Lived in Fiji for several years and learned "how to be independent of mom"
- Serves on several organizational boards
- Enjoys reading books about social justice, civil rights, and inclusion

My story is interesting because I am non-speaking and autistic, and I am happy with who I am. I know that may seem strange but I am living my best life. I have a loving family and I can go places with my friends. I get good support from my aides and therapists. I have a loving church family and I have good doctors to take care of me. I am learning new things and I am becoming more independent.

I felt accomplished when I lived in Fiji because I had to live without my mom telling me what to do all the time. I was fourteen years old. I managed to function without communicating by listening to everything and following directions. I did this for two years. Now that I can communicate I want to say I appreciate everything they did for me. I learned how to swim, ride horses, and bless my food, and how to be independent of mom. I talked to mom using Skype. I would read to her and show her my school work.

A big accomplishment since I learned to spell to communicate is having an opportunity to learn and take regular classes. I finally can demonstrate that I am smart and can learn new things. My autism does not mean that I am stupid. It does not mean that I cannot learn. It means simply that I cannot learn in traditional ways. I learn by listening and I communicate by spelling. My mom reads to me. We are reading What the Truth Sounds like by Michael Eric Dyson. It is about racial injustice in America. I am interested in social justice for all people. The disability community can learn a lot from the civil rights movement. It's all about inclusion.

Spelling to communicate has helped me to be an advocate. Before I could communicate my mom always spoke for me in individualized educational plan (IEP) meetings and school board meetings. Now that I can communicate I can advocate for myself and advocate for others. I serve on several organizational boards and can participate in discussions about issues that affect me.

I want to have my own apartment and I want to go to college to study art history. I will need support with money management and with communication. I can do a lot of things, like make my lunch, wash dishes, fold my laundry and make my bed. I know how to keep myself clean and dress appropriately.

My advice to younger generations who don't speak: Be happy. Keep learning. Keep fighting for your right to an education. Make every day count. My advice to a parent of a nonspeaking child: Keep fighting for your child. You are their voice. They depend on you. Be patient. Keep talking to them. They are listening. Don't be embarrassed by your child's behaviors. Presume competence.

I pray that God will bless me with a healthy life, and love, and happiness.

Reflection Questions:
1. Ben lived in Fiji for two years and learned many new skills without having to depend on his mom. If you were to choose a location any where in the world to leave for a couple of years, where would it be? Which skills would you work on without your caretaker there?
2. Ben serves on organizational boards to provide his input on decisions that the organizations make. On which organizations' boards would you desire to serve? What kind of input would you give them?

46 NICO NAVARRO

Nico Navarro
California
17 years old

Highlights:
- Has experienced full educational inclusion and is an advocate for public policy and community inclusion
- Has presented about his experiences at universities and national conferences

When I was little, everyone just assumed that I had an intellectual disability because I was always acting autistic and I was not able to communicate. I always felt like I was the only person in the world like me who was smart but could not tell anyone. I was trapped in my own mind and trying to break free of my head. It was very sad and lonely for me. I really wanted to tell everyone that I was smart and that I could read and do math, but I wasn't able to tell anyone. I was acting out, getting in trouble, and sad all the time trying to let people know that I was in there in my head ready to come out. I did not always understand that I had autism. I thought maybe I had an intellectual disability too. I was ready to give up and stay in my own world until my awesome special education teacher taught me to type using facilitated communication. I was so happy that day. I ran out of the room signing 'happy' and my teacher was crying she was so happy. I could not believe that I could communicate. I had been trapped in my own world for 10 long years and now I was free. I showed everyone that I was smart and had learned everything taught to me in my classes. Fortunately, I had been fully included my whole life so I had access to general education along with my friends. I was ready to teach others to fight for their right to be fully included.

I left my charter school and moved to high school. I was afraid that the other kids would not accept me and the teachers would not want me in their classes. For the most part, high school has been awesome. The kids are really cool to me and hang out with me at lunch. Most teachers have been wary of working with me but have accepted me in their classes. I have had people who do not believe in facilitated communication and had administrators trying to deny me the right to be fully included, but my awesome parents would not let that happen. I am grateful to them for always fighting for my rights. I sometimes feel it would be easier for me to not be in general education classes, but I need to prove to the administration at my school that kids with disabilities should be included. Many of my friends with disabilities are not included and it makes me very upset. I feel that all students should be taught together. I feel lucky to be included and hope that my success will pave the way for others. I want all kids with disabilities to have a voice and be included.

I am 18 years old and graduated high school. I want to go to junior college after I graduate from high school. I want to study psychology and literature. I will work hard to get a degree. I want to be an advocate for people with disabilities, write in my blog, stay aware of legislation regarding people with disabilities to make changes to policies, and present at conferences. I probably will try to write a book myself someday about my life and present to the world that people with disabilities are valuable members of our society.

I am dedicated to fighting for the rights of all people with disabilities to be fully included. I have done a lot for others. I have spoken at CSUN numerous times to teaching credential students, presented at TASH and Cal-TASH conferences, received an award from a State Legislator, written a letter to ASHA in support of facilitated communication, and had a story written about me in the local newspaper. I will continue the fight for inclusion for others when I go to college next year and throughout my life.

Reflection Questions:
1. Despite experiencing much support for inclusion, Nico's parents had to advocate for his right to his communication method and inclusion in school. Who are the people in your life who have stepped up for you to fight for your rights? What did they help you accomplish?
2. Nico has presented at conferences and desires to stay informed about legislation and policies that affect people with disabilities. Why do you think activism that centers on policy-making is important? How would you get started in educating yourself about federal, state, or local policies?

ABOUT THE EDITOR

Edlyn Vallejo Peña, Ph.D. is the chair and associate professor of the doctoral program in education leadership at California Lutheran University. She is also the co-founder and director of the Autism and Communication Center. Dr. Peña's scholarship and advocacy focus on supporting the transition and success of autistic college students, as well the communication rights of nonspeaking and minimally speaking autistics. Her edited book, *Communication Alternatives in Autism: Perspectives on Typing and Spelling Approaches for the Nonspeaking* (2019), features ten prominent autistic individuals who advocate for communication and inclusion rights. For more information, please visit www.edlynpena.com and www.callutheran.edu/autism.